Why We Hurt
and
Who Can Heal

John C. Cooper

Why We Hurt
and
Who Can Heal

John C. Cooper

WORD BOOKS
PUBLISHER
4800 WEST WACO DRIVE
WACO, TEXAS
76703

For Ann
in thanks for twenty-four years,
four children,
a thousand setbacks, and a few successes

Love begins
in that territory
that lies beyond
yours and mine
in a country called ours
Above the level of competition
and ambition
on the high plains
that know nothing
of victory or defeat.

Love flows from the melting
glaciers of the self
to mingle with the unnamed waters
of others
to lose itself in the mighty river
that fertilizes lands and years
unselfishly
making life that it may never see
reality.

Contents

Preface

Like so many other pastors or professors of religion, I was fortunate enough to have outstanding theologians as friends and teachers. I continually benefit by the opportunities that were mine as a student, during a dozen years of higher education, of knowing and learning from Abdel Ross Wentz, the great Lutheran Church historian, and of knowing Roland Bainton, the outstanding biographer of Luther. I will always be grateful for the opportunity I had of being the student of Paul Tillich, the famous systematic theologian, and of Mircea Eliade, the leading scholar of the History of Religions field.

However, one man, now gone to his reward, returns in my thoughts every time life gets complex, my blood-sugar level is low, and I seriously question whether I can cope with my duties and anxieties. That man is Joseph Haroutunian, a Reformed Theologian, Calvin scholar, and demanding teacher. Haroutunian taught me and others to expect problems and to deal with them rather than becoming discouraged. Old "Joe" (as we called him behind his back) once retorted, when I spoke of various opportunities I had: "All I have are problems!" Unfortunately, it took me several more years of maturity to see that Joe was right—and all I had were "problems," too.

Joe knew, before I did, that we all hurt, sometimes, and that some of us hurt all the time. Life is not easy nor does it necessarily become easier as we grow older or more spiritual. Martin Luther is reported to have remarked that all his problems started the day he became a Christian. Faith in Christ doesn't solve problems, but rather puts problems in a new light, and by the brightness of that new light often reveals to us many problems (such as the needs of others) that we didn't know we had before conversion. "All I have are problems" is not cynicism or unbelief speaking, but it is the very voice of Christian maturity.

This book is an exercise in discussing these problems, which can be areas of hurt, in every Christian's life and of trying to understand how we can grow by dealing faithfully with them. If you will tell me where you hurt, I'll tell you what is hurting me and together we'll examine what God may be trying to tell us in these hurts of every day.

Many books have been touted as having the power of increasing human happiness. We are told that just by reading them and putting their suggestions into practice, we will be happier. This book makes no such claim. Rather, my aim and claim is more modest, and being a bearer of smaller promise may, hopefully, deliver more of what it claims than have its less modest competitors. The theme of this book is simply that all of us are chronically nagged, from time to time, by a sense of human hurt, a feeling of sadness that is not easily explained. Ironically, it is not necessarily the realistic sense of pain of the poverty worn, the ill, or the mentally upset that I mean, but the dull ache of spiritual hurt that plagues the most well-to-do, healthy, adjusted lives. This is a book about human hurt, the kind of hurt we do to ourselves and to each other—and that others do to us.

You may feel that you can survive without a book on such a theme. "After all," you may think, "life is hard enough without searching out the nuggets of unhappiness deep inside me." You might think that, but you wouldn't be correct. To live fully, to greet every day as a new start, to search out and find that elusive human good called happiness, is what life is all about—and happiness is not found by the denial of hurt, but by triumph over it.

In short, if you find life hard enough already, you need this book rather than a positive thinking volume that will encourage you to forget that silent ache in the depths of your life. If the psychoanalytic movement made any human contribution, it was to give us the insight that denial and repression of feelings and pain are a recipe for illness and unhappiness, not for triumphant living.

One sunny early September morning, I was walking from the dormitory to the waterfront of a lovely Methodist camp, where our seminary was holding a retreat. Hurrying to join a study group of students on the beach, I looked up suddenly when my name was called. With surprise I noted one of the past-June graduates. "Why, what's up? I thought you graduated, Jim," I said. "Sure, I did," the young man answered. "I just came by to ask if you would preach my ordination sermon." I was flabbergasted. This young fellow and I were worlds apart theologically, but I liked him, and I was touched by his request. "Of course, I'll preach for you. When do you want it done?"

Some time later the ordination service was held. Everything went well. I felt honored to be a part of this significant event. Even later, I found out why *I* was asked to be the speaker. "Jim thought you were the only appropriate preacher," another friend told me. "After all, you taught him that Christianity essentially means forgiveness, and he believed that. So since you had forgiven him after so many theological arguments, and he had forgiven you, the decision was obvious."

And the decision was profoundly right. Christianity is a matter of forgiveness. If forgiveness is hard to give sometimes, that only proves the point. Someone once remarked:

"There's no use burying the hatchet if you're going to put up a marker in its place."

Forgiveness must be complete, and to be so we must be willing to face up to how we have hurt each other and work through the hurt.

I am convinced that our culture is making little progress toward the cultivation of deep human happiness. Why? Because North Americans tend to "go around" difficulties rather than through them—denying shortcomings rather than admitting them and seeking to set them right. Our usual American life style is to maintain harmony by denying the little things that bother us for months and years. Then, one day that huge build-up of psychic hurt explodes in a tantrum, a strike, a fight, or a divorce. Somehow, mature Christians, who follow a Lord who conquered the world by going through suffering, the cross, rejection, pain, and death, ought to know better.

This book is an invitation to work through the places where we hurt to find a happiness based on acceptance, not on denial, on forgiveness, not on gain, and on God, not on the world alone.

Welcome to reflection on where we hurt and to what our hurts can teach us about ourselves and those around us.

JOHN CHARLES COOPER

Findlay, Ohio

The Frantic Search
for Happiness

The Frantic Search for Happiness

The songs of the common people, the jokes they tell, the graffiti they write upon the thousands of walls across the landscape, tell us, as dreams do, of the inner meaning of human experience. In their very earthiness and triviality, popular songs and slogans spray-painted on subway walls inform us of what is truly happening in the minds and emotions of everyday, average people. The wise have always understood this. Isaiah prepared signs to wear upon back and chest (like the "sandwich" signs men used to wear while walking up and down the street), and wrote prophecies of doom for Jerusalem in big letters on them. Isaiah put the truth "out front" in a common but striking way, so that "he may run who reads it" (Hab. 2:2; also see Isa. 8:1 and 30:8). Even so, Carl Gustav Jung, the great psychiatrist, had his patients keep a record of their dreams, as did Sigmund Freud. "Doodling" and dreaming are ways in which the inner meaning of human events announce themselves to us, if we are wise enough to listen.

With this in mind, we can understand what a friend of mine meant, during the Watergate hearings, when he saw an anti-Nixon graffiti in a public lavatory and said, "Nixon

is doomed." We can also understand the insight of Karl
Barth, who dreamed that he died and went to heaven
pushing a wheelbarrow full of his theological writings. In
his dream Barth heard St. Peter say, "You can come in, but
not with all this." The graffiti announced, to the sensitive,
that the common people were "on" to Nixon's behavior.
The dream announced to the wise old Barth that Christ was
his Savior, not by any works of his own, including dozens of
fine books on Christian theology.

If we keep our outer eyes open, and the eyes of our spirit
attuned to the inner light, we can find messages from God
dropped in the street all around us, as the poet Walt Whit-
man once observed.

In 1963, I had my clearest experience with the problems
involved in trying to keep career and marriage in harmoni-
ous working arrangement. My problem grew painful when I
left my wife and children "safe" in South Carolina and
traveled to Chicago to complete my studies for the Ph.D.
degree. I thought (we thought!) the whole process would be
simpler that way. In actuality, it was a miserable arrangement for me. Professor Joseph Haroutunian noted that I was
moping about the Divinity School and called me to his
office one day. "What's wrong with you?" he asked. "I'm
lonely," was all I could say. Then I explained my predica-
ment. "But life's too short for anything like that," Joe said.
"Do something about it." It seemed that a bright light
dawned on me—I *should*, I *could* do something about the
situation. "I'll go home this weekend and bring my family
here," I said. "Do it," was Joe's last word.

Moving a wife and three small children from a new
two-story home in a quiet Southern town to a one-room,
dirty apartment in a big city ghetto was not easy. But it was
possible, and more, it was possible by sacrifice, to hold
career activity and home life together. My work and family
were still problems to deal with in Chicago, but not as big a
problem as that caused by separation.

14

That readjustment of where we hurt was relatively simple. Severe problems of career conflict of either husband or wife or both can be much more painful and difficult to adjust.

Long before the birth of Christ, reflective men and women thought long upon the meaning of human happiness. Among the ancient Greeks, the several philosophical schools each taught a different interpretation of life and pointed toward a different life style as the way to happiness.

The ancient ways of looking at life and the pursuit of happiness are still very much alive, even as we approach the twenty-first century of the Christian era.

Plato, following the great Socrates, taught that man's true happiness lay in the cultivation of the soul. The soul, while linked to God and the hereafter in Plato's thought, was chiefly understood as intellect. For this reason, Plato taught that happiness, in the truest sense, was available only to the intellectual, possible only for the philosopher. To become happy, Plato thought one must cut himself off from love of human beings and long for heaven.

Aristotle, going his own way and developing his philosophy in contrast to his teacher, Plato, felt that happiness was a much more worldly affair. In terms modern Americans would not find hard to understand, Aristotle taught that a person must have enough wealth to be satisfied physically and mentally, must have good health, good friends and civic honor to be genuinely happy. Not only this, but long life, too, is needed for true happiness. Aristotle declared that we cannot think that those who die young achieve happiness. The essential element in Aristotle's vision of the happy life is, therefore, maturity. Aristotle saw all the possibilities of life as potentially present in the young person, but he felt that only time and hard work could realize these potentials and create true happiness. Anything that interfered with one's self-realization caused the person hurt.

When we hear the old saying, "Only the good die

young," we misunderstand it, for it means that good people, no matter how old they are, are young at heart. My father, for example, says that he has a 20-year-old mind in a 77-year-old body.

The Stoics, a wide-ranging group of moral philosophers who were still active during New Testament times, felt that absolute world-denial was the way to happiness. Not to want anything, to be perfectly neutral about material things, honor, and society is the Stoic vision of happiness. Like Buddha, the Stoic philosopher saw clearly that the root of suffering is desire. The harsh answer to suffering, then, was not to desire anything. This philosophy produced many noble men, but, at the least, we can see that it is a little like throwing the baby out with the bath water. Marcus Aurelius, an emperor of Rome, followed this philosophy and lived like a common soldier in the field during his reign.

The Epicureans were another philosophical sect who tackled the problems of human happiness. It may seem a bit ludicrous, at first glance, but Epicurus taught that the secret of happiness was a good digestion. Epicurus pointed out that while a person may have everything in the world, a simple case of upset stomach can make him quite unhappy. Of course, Epicurus was a wise man and he was using "good digestion" as a symbol to point to the need for calm and balance in one's life. Epicurus took his own advice, retired to a pleasant garden with his pupils, drank only water, and ate only plain porridge in an effort to preserve the balance of his digestion and life. Epicurus taught that men should have many acquaintances, but refrain from close friendships and from the passions of love and hate. To like anything or anyone is to court unhappiness. Once more, the baby went tumbling out with the bath water.

The coming of Christianity produced a new approach to the problem of happiness. While there were many suggestions as to the meaning of happiness in the Scriptures and in early Christian history, a major theme in every Christian vision was: Happiness is to live in accord with the will of God for one's life. While such a teaching is incontrovertible, a problem arises when one attempts to determine just what God's will for him really is. We will be discussing this question in this book, but the simplest answer is that God wants us to enjoy life and to be a blessing to other people, too.

One philosophy of happiness was popular among some groups of people both in the ancient Greek and later Christian period—and is still with us today. This was and is the philosophy of hedonism—the no-holds-barred search for pleasure.

Both Plato, through the teaching of Socrates in the *Dialogues,* and Aristotle examined and rejected the idea that the good for man was physical pleasure. The Stoics and the Epicureans also criticized this notion. Poor old Epicurus, the most upright of men, has unfortunately been saddled with the charge that he taught men to seek physical pleasure—a charge which is simply untrue.

There *were* hedonistic (pleasure-seeking) philosophers, however. Many of these teachers were active during the Roman period and their doctrines were attacked by the early Christians. The idea that "if it feels good, do it," is far older than the present-day "Playboy Philosophy." The Bible rather roundly denounces the idea, "Eat and drink, for tomorrow we die" (1 Cor. 15:32). Not only sanctified reason but plain human common sense can easily see the fallacy of hedonism. Pleasure sought too avidly becomes pain. The pleasure-seeker soon becomes jaded and unable to receive the same sensations he once did from sex, food, and drink. Far beyond this is the insight that such hedonism is unredeemedly selfish, caring for no one but the solitary self. Hedonism is unredeemedly selfish and it is a prescription for ultimate unhappiness, not happiness.

Apart from every religious and philosophical consideration, human beings do seek happiness for themselves and

17

for those they love. It is not a game, then, to ask, "Just what is the happiness we seek?" Through the centuries people's answers have fallen into several easily identifiable categories:

Happiness is the attainment of all the pleasures you can have in life, and the avoidance of life's pain.

Happiness is being of service to others, being needed, as citizen, parent, and friend.

Happiness is preparation for an eternal life beyond this world.

Happiness is the full flowering of the self, in all its creative possibilities. It is the identification of and development of one's unique personality.

This last view is the single most prevalent conception of happiness today. As Tom Wolfe, the journalist, has it, we belong to the "Me" generation. Everyone seems to want to talk about "Me" and to search for the real "Me." Happiness, for so many of us, is always having our self as the center of everyone's attention. Yet, the experiences of life seem to teach us that happiness is something other than physical pleasure or even the stroking of the ego. Happiness does have a spiritual, a serving element, without which we never know what happiness is. Consider this story.

"Is Everybody Happy?"

Acrid smoke bit into my nostrils, burning its way through the ice in my mustache, but I moved closer to the fire in the oil drum. I was cold, cold beyond description. We had been fighting in the frozen mountains of North Korea for more than a month. Dirty snow whipped past our ears at high velocity, dropping the temperature even lower than the official 35° below zero, Fahrenheit. The several layers of clothes I was wearing were so stiff I could hardly move. A middle-aged sergeant with a wicked leer looked around our miserable group and laughed fiendishly. "Is everybody happy?" he cried. And the funny thing was that we all smiled. We were cold, dirty, tired, and hungry, and most of all, scared, yet we weren't unhappy. I know that I was in physical agony, but I wasn't sad. Somehow, as in the midst of a brutal football scrimmage or during a grueling boxing match, a person can be exhausted and in pain, and yet be happy. I learned that in 1950 as we marched out of North Korea.

The Bible observes that a strong man rejoices to run a race and that a person will punish his body to prepare for a contest, even if the prize is only a wreath that withers in an afternoon. External circumstances may bring us suffering, but that suffering does not necessarily make us unhappy. *Happiness and unhappiness are conditions of the human spirit, not states of the organism.*

Need I belabor this point? In every city there are families living in fine homes, driving new cars, belonging to country clubs, warm, fed, and praised, who are besieged with continual unhappiness. The men may drink too much. The children may be drifting aimlessly. The women may be considering divorce. Everything that supposedly makes for human happiness is there, yet the happiness for which people reach exceeds their grasp. Happiness is a matter of the inner life, not of the external world.

Happiness lies hidden, ready for us to find it, in the deep things of the Spirit we so regularly ignore. The acrid smoke of our burning dreams still bites our nostrils, and the freezing sleet of our inner loneliness still stings our faces. But if the inner man is strong, we can still laugh and declare ourselves happy. And suddenly, in the shock of our recognition of the healthy spirit who lives behind the twisted smile of our fellow sufferer, we know that we are happy, since happiness is simply saying "yes" to life. Not weakness of body, but weakness of spirit makes us sad.

As I write these words I see, in my mind's eye, the figure of a youthful, boyish second lieutenant of Marines walking

19

from one huddled group to another. His name is Newton and everyone calls him "Fig Newton." Newton has just been cracking jokes with the small group of British Marine commandos who are marching with us. "You know," he cries, "I asked them for cocoa and all they've got is tea! Can you imagine that, tea! One of them told me not even the queen has got cocoa!" "Ain't nobody got no cocoa, Newton?" somebody shouts. "Even the blooming queen ain't got cocoa," Newton replies.

From then on whenever things were bad or we lacked anything—which was often—someone would shout, "Even the queen ain't got cocoa," and we would laugh.

The world is hard, but humor and friendship can soften its hardest edges. That, to me, is happiness.

A Sense of Loss We Know Not Why

Henry David Thoreau once wrote that most people live lives of quiet desperation. That may be an exaggeration, but unhappiness is fairly common among adults. Pastors spend much time counseling church members and non-members who have problems. Psychiatrists and psychologists do a land-office business. Mental health centers and family service agencies are overtaxed. Whether we are quietly desperate or not, many of us do seem to have a sense of loss, although we may not know why.

It is much too easy to offer standard religious answers designed to fit everyone, and consequently fitting no one, to people who feel this sense of loss, of hurt. Such answers really answer nothing, since we can hear answers only to questions which we ask ourselves. Something is amiss in many of our lives, but the lack of "rightness" differs from person to person. To speak of sin is necessary and we will do so here, but in the theological, not the moral sense. We are all sinners, in rebellion against God, but we are not so easily categorized as guilty and innocent in the moral realm. Our problems of hurt, of nostalgia for we know not what, involve pain—and that pain must be overcome first, before advice can be given and heeded. One thing is fact, people who hurt must change, but the big questions are "how?" and "in what directions?"

Perhaps if we understand a bit about our total life cycles, the normal pattern in which our lives fall, we may see some of our answer.

If madness is defined as a sense of the loss of control over our own lives, of being at the mercy of unconscious, or extrapersonal forces, then most of us today are mad. (Many social commentators agree.) We intuitively sense that here is a gap between what we actually are and really do in the world and what we inwardly want ourselves to be and to do. Paul described this gap in Romans 7:19: "For I do not do the good I want, but the evil I do not want is what I do."

This gap is the psychic locus of what theology calls "sin." Evil is the perverse seeking of good (building up) that results in the not good (tearing down) occurring. Sin is the psychic separation, the alienation between those feelings and actions which promote life and the expressions of those feelings and actions in such a way that life is harmed, not helped. "To do evil that good may come" is not misguided zeal, it is the very essence of sin. As T. S. Eliot said: "The last temptation is the greatest treason, to do the right thing for the wrong reason."

Madness comes upon us when the world we inhabit falls apart. Man does not have an environment, as an animal does. Rather, he has a world. Our world is not just a physical thing, it is the result of a *Weltanschauung*, a world-view. In the final sense, we produce the kind of world we inhabit— our values, our desires are prior to our knowledge of the world. We know what we want to know; what we do not want to know, we do not even recognize. Long ago, Aristotle recognized the polarity of inward receptivity and outward stimulus; only what we are set to grasp can be grasped. This is illustrated by prejudice—we do not even see instances of goodness in people of races or nations or classes we dislike. Our values determine what we can know.

There are a number of familiar social-psychological situations that provide negative instances, "backward proof" of the priority of values over facts in the knowing process. Like it or not, what we feel about the world, how we see the world (in terms of world-view or outlook, often represented by the German term *Weltanschauung*) determines what we see, what we find in the world. This may not be universally true, but its popularity as a knowledge-gathering method calls in question any strict insistence upon a classic value-free empiricism.

The first example is drawn from human prejudice. Whites who belittle Blacks may be participants in a society where many Blacks are responsible citizens—moral, industrious, and intelligent. However, these prejudiced persons see only Black irresponsibility, immorality, and laziness. They see what they expect to see, what their "values" tell them the world is like. In similar fashion, radical Blacks see all whites as exploitative and radical; anti-Communists see Red plots everywhere, from the waterworks to the legislative hall.

The second example is drawn from human emotions, particularly those of hate and love. A person who actively dislikes someone infrequently recognizes good qualities and noble actions on the part of the person he hates. A man or woman "in love" rarely notices the warts on the beloved until the passion passes. We see a reflected image of our inward values when we look upon the face of the enemy or the form of the beloved. The field of literature is our record of human folly.

The third example is drawn from human needs. Plato recognized the "passions" or "appetites" as an element in the makeup of the human soul. We are all aware of the changes in personality and the thinking process brought on

22

by strong sexual excitation or by an unrelenting feeling of hunger or thirst. When one is fully nourished and in a good state of self-possession, he takes notice of the world around him, of the beauty of the sky, of the nature of the countryside he is passing through, of the faces of other people. But when he is sexually aroused his intension is narrowed down to the proverbial "main thing." When a group of us offered a course in pornography and sexuality at Bowling Green University in Ohio, in 1972, we began by giving the participants a little test involving their responses to 100 photographs taken from American magazines. Each student was tested separately and asked to check whether the photo spoke to him/her of sex, "not at all; a little; a moderate amount, or a lot." One young man checked that a photo of a can of tomato soup spoke to him of sex "a lot." When asked why, he replied that he was "horny" and in that condition everything spoke to him of sex! I suspect that he was not an atypical case. Facts are distorted completely out of context when the organism insists upon its needs. These organic movements become overarching values, or value-facts, that take priority over everything else. Anyone who has taken a written examination while hungry recognizes the truth of this statement.

The geography of evil is everywhere. Evil and good occur together, being twins born of every human dream, idea, life style, or action. The biblical stories of Cain and Abel, Jacob and Esau, Isaac and Ishmael, and Joseph and his brothers all illustrate this point. "As ugly as homemade sin" is an old proverb that points to the rise of sin within the same context as the expression of love. The wheat and the tares grow up together as long as history lasts.

Dr. Karl Menninger, the celebrated psychiatrist, has suggested that many of our modern day hurts are disguised as the result of illnesses when they are actually caused by sin. In his book, *Whatever Became of Sin?*, Dr. Menninger discusses what is wrong with our society, the disappearance of the idea of sin, the new social morality, the redefining of sin as crime and as symptom, sin as collective responsibility, and the seven deadly sins.[1] It is certainly "different" today, for anyone, doctor of medicine or doctor of theology, to credit human hurt to the effect of sin, but it is actually to the point.

The Christian must speak that word, *sin*. But the Christian must not speak moralistically; he or she must speak theologically, i.e., not from a position of ethics, but from a position of faith. In Dietrich Bonhoeffer's words, we must not speak to a sin-filled world from the position of abstract, unreal, moral principle, but from the place of the incarnate word of God in concrete reality. Then we shall speak about the real reasons we hurt, and not in unhelpful terms. For example, the Christian will say, "Putting your hand in that fire has burned you"; he will not say "fire burns." We are called to point out the concrete, the real, so that God may forgive real sin through the reality of Christ.

Sin, when mentioned as the cause of our everyday, lifelong problems, frankly sounds scary—and a bit fanatical—today. It may, nevertheless, be true that we have the nagging hurts and fears we do precisely because we refuse to face up to sin as a problem. Sin is a standard word and concept in the Christian tradition—as well as in the Jewish and Moslem religions. Basically it means revolt against God, resistance to the Divine Will. Sin is a matter of the spirit, accomplished through the will; it is not primarily a matter of the flesh or the natural passions.

Christians should know that sin is a constant companion of life. We are born with a tendency to prefer our own will over that of our Maker (original sin) and go on to do very real sins at every point in our lives. Anything that is not done out of true faith in God and in love is sinful. We can and should ask for God's forgiveness through Christ continually, but we know we will sin again, no matter how hard we try not to do so. We are all tempted, although we pray in

24

the Lord's Prayer that we will be led through temptation without falling prey to it. To be temptable is not in itself sinful, of course, but is the very condition of human morality.

Traditionally, there are seven deadly sins, although the number varies from theologian to theologian, and it seems clear that there are more serious sins than only seven. The ancient list, with some updates and expansion, includes:

1. Envy (hate, conspiracy, dejection, low self-image, lack of self-esteem)
2. Anger (violence, aggression, vindictiveness, revenge, cruelty)
3. Pride (vainglory, biogotry, spiritual pride, egocentric- • ity, selfishness)
4. Sloth (laziness, *acedia*, boredom, *ennui*)
5. Avarice (affluence, dishonesty, stealing, cheating, ingratitude)
6. Gluttony (waste, luxury living, drunkenness, obesity, drug addiction)
7. Lust (infidelity, adultery, fornication, pornography)

Some of these sins are included in every one of our personal and social hurts. Becoming aware of what we might be doing to resist God's will and to insist on our own may well help us to escape from self-hurting behavior.

By all means, I do not mean to make you feel guilty by speaking of sin. Guilt is the most painful of all hurts— precisely because it is not focused on reality—on the reality of sin and the ever-present possibility of God's forgiveness. We would not suffer from guilt if we really recognized our sinfulness and confessed to Almighty God. No amount of suffering from guilt can ever change anyone for the better.

Following up this insight of seeing sin as a basis for human hurt, and Christ as its ultimate healing, consider this long letter written by the mystery novelist and Christian apologist, Dorothy L. Sayers:

. . . the "story" of Crucified God appears irrelevant because people nowadays have no sense of sin. . . . I'm a
very poor person to appreciate modern man's feelings in all
this, because I can't think of any personal misfortunes
which have befallen me which were not, in one way or
another, my own fault. I don't mean this necessarily in the
profounder and more religious sense, I mean that I know
jolly well that if anything unpleasant has happened to me in
my life, I had usually "asked for it." Consequently, when I
talk about carrying the sins of the world, "I'm going outside
my experience—anything I have to put up with looks to me
like the direct punishment for my *own* sins, and not to leave
much margin over for the redemption of other peoples."
But I do see that most people do look upon themselves as
the victims of undeserved misfortunes, which they have
done nothing to provoke. Contemporary literature and
thought seem to be steeped in self-pity, which is the most
enervating state of mind imaginable.

If only they could start from the idea that there is "something funny about man"—and that he does tend to fight
against the right order of things, they could get a more robust
outlook on suffering and catastrophes, and see that they were
carrying:

a) the direct consequence of their wrongness—the "punitive
element" in suffering
b) the indirect consequence of other people's wrongness—
the "redemptive" element . . .

I remember Alan Wheatley saying "I can't bear all this
killing—it's so *irrevocable.*" All death is irrevocable, that's
why we find it such an outrage. . . . There isn't any
"escape" or "fresh start" in the sense of *abolishing* the past
and its consequences. The past can never be wiped out but
only redeemed and "made good." To *escape* from the past
would mean Christ coming down from the Cross; to redeem
the past means going through the Cross to the Resurrection.
One muddle about forgiveness is of the same kind—
forgiveness is the restoration of a good relationship, but it
doesn't abolish the consequence of the offence, nor is it going
back to where we were before the offence was committed, it's
got to be a new relationship. . . . If I borrow money from

you and squander it, your forgiving the debt doesn't put back the money—that's lost, and you bear the loss and so "carry the guilt." If I get in a rage with you and throw your best teapot out of the window, no amount of forgiveness will unbreak the teapot—all we can aim for is a relationship in which both you *and* I can bear to sit down and breakfast together out of a shaving mug without feeling uncomfortable and without an ostentatious avoidance of the subject of teapots. . . . .

I think it's here that the relevancy of the Cross comes in—that the power which made and sustains the Universe, with its iron laws is the Power that (not prevents evil from happening, which would make freedom of choice unmeaning, but) makes evil good . . ." [2]

The great Swiss theologian, Emil Brunner, also wrote in *The Word of God and Modern Man* [3] about the hurt in life that comes from guilt—which is the result of sin. Brunner declares that we are bound to our unchangeable past by our guilt, when we could be free of that guilt if we would simply ask God's forgiveness through Jesus Christ.

Psychologist Wayne W. Dyer also treats this issue, although purely from a psychological perspective, in his best-selling book, *Your Erroneous Zones*. [4] Dyer tells us that guilt and worry cause us hurt in the present by a failure of our wills to put the past behind us and to live openly toward the future. Guilt is the way in which we spoil the present moment by concern over the past, which we cannot change, and worry is the way we destroy our present by conjuring up false visions of the future—which is also beyond our control.

Sin thus cuts both ways, bracketing our present moment with guilt about the past and worry about the future, in the manner in which artillery brackets an army position with shells falling on both sides. As long as sin is not recognized and is not offered up to God for his forgiveness, that sinfulness has the power to destroy every possibility of happiness we have in this present moment God has given us.

27

WHY WE HURT AND WHO CAN HEAL

Loneliness and Frustration

If there is a sense of loss in our lives, a feeling of hurt that we cannot fully understand, the possibility is great that this sense arises most clearly in our conscious feelings of loneliness and frustration. This loneliness may be felt as a deep pain, even though we live in the midst of a family and work in a busy office. It is a feeling, somehow, of not really being known, of not truthfully being part of the groups around us. Of course, we may, in fact, be lonely in a physical sense as well. Perhaps we are widowed or divorced, or are forced by the nature of our job to travel constantly. In this case, it is a reenforcement of loneliness both in the outer as well as the inner sense.

Another typical area of life that reveals the inner hurt is frustration.

Perhaps we can see frustration most clearly in a simpler creature. A rat runs frantically through a maze, finding one dead end after another. The animal tries this pathway, then that one, then another, all to no avail. The experimental psychologists have stacked the deck against the poor beast— there is no way out of the maze. After a while the rat begins to move erratically. It seems to have lost the ability to proceed normally. Moving aimlessly and more and more slowly, the creature is disoriented and soon loses interest. It huddles into its own skin, giving up on the whole enterprise.

We would say that this rat is frustrated. It has beaten its head against the stone wall of its situation and gotten nowhere. Inside, the rat's emotions are seething. It is filled with rage and hurt, but that rage is now directed toward itself. Such a level of stress leaves the rat paralyzed, out of touch with reality. All the beast can do is to huddle and look stupidly straight ahead.

People get frustrated, too. Human beings, confronted with problems, begin to break down emotionally inside,

28

when all their efforts to relieve pain end in bitter failure. We try and try and try again, but even the best of us run out of "tries" eventually. Frustration can lead, then, even in the highly intelligent human being, to paralysis—or just short of this—to aggression and hurt if someone triggers a psychic explosion within us. An intensely angry person may be walking around unconsciously looking for someone "to blow up" with.

Frustration is related to boredom in the human being. Both negative conditions point toward something spiritual and transcendent in human nature which is being denied and demonized by hurtful events and relationships. Frustration would not be possible if man were not created with the ability to have fellowship with other people and with God.

Frustration like loneliness is an inner state. There is a real sense in which we feel loneliness, boredom, and frustration all together. Frustration is that feeling that somehow all our best intentions are warped. It's the conclusion that all our hopes are vain dreams. It is a sense of passing judgment on ourselves and that judgment is failure.

Perhaps no hurt in life is stronger than this sense of inward failure. Out of it flows all kinds of unhappiness. A sense of inferiority, an inability to make decisions because of lack of trust in oneself, a deeply burning anger, stress, guilt, grief, panic, and anxiety over the feeling that our life will soon be over and be wasted, all grow out of frustration.

Since this is true we need to ask ourselves, what causes frustration? Once we ask the question, two classic answers come to mind. The first answer is that our expectations are too high. We want too much. We try to fly too close to the sun. We fail because of an overweening pride. When our natural talents and opportunities do not prove able to support our grandiose dreams, we fall into self-doubt, into anger with our circumstances—in short, into frustration that can lead on to despair.

There is a second classic answer: We are frustrated because we do not hope enough. Settling too early into a comfortable rut, we do not reach out far enough. We are thoughtless in our younger years and consequently do not foresee that with maturity our powers will unfold and make us capable of higher things than we suspected when we were young. This kind of frustration arises when a man comes to understand that his intelligence is higher than he thought earlier and that he has an interest and ability in philosophy or art, but he has locked himself into a job repairing cars or selling insurance. In the case of a woman, in youth she may, with little forethought, enter into marriage and the rearing of children, and later find that she would like to pursue a career. Here, larger dreams in middle life cause frustration because the person elected smaller dreams in earlier life. The problem in this world is that our dreams become concrete. We build walls around our lives that enclose a space only as large as we can imagine that we should claim for ourselves. This situation is quite well-known with married women today, since this kind of frustration is part of the fuel that drives the feminist movement to attempt to change the structure of our society.

Both classic answers concerning the cause of frustration thus turn on the size of our dreams and the courage of our hopes. When our dreams are larger than our ability—that is, when they are unrealistic with reference to what is within us—we bruise ourselves against the reality of the world later. When our dreams are not large enough, we wound ourselves later in life as a kind of self-punishment for not believing fully in ourselves as young people. In both cases, pain is the result. There is another sense in which both these classic answers for frustration are really the *same* answer. Both of them assume that we really do not know ourselves. In a deep way, both dreams that are too grand and hopes that are not grand enough grow out of a failure to truly know ourselves. The pain that frustration brings is thus a penalty for being out of touch with reality. As Socrates said some 2400 years ago: "The unexamined life is not worth living." He declared that we must know ourselves. Our first duty to ourselves and others involves self-reflection. We must investigate what is truly within us and what we genuinely want to do before slipping easily into an arrangement with the world that is comfortable at the time, but that lacks the space for growth needed in a life that is lived fully and completely.

I've written of the need to know ourselves elsewhere. I suggest in my book, *Fantasy and the Human Spirit*,[5] that our culture encourages us not to be reflective, not to really consider who we are, and what we would like to be. I strongly feel that much of our unhappiness arises from and consequently, much social harm is done because we do not know who we are. By being cut off from our real selves, we can never be truly satisfied. By not paying attention to our innermost desires, we live by the rules and wishes of others around us. This means that we satisfy others or a social role, but never do we truly satisfy ourselves. The source of much of our hurt, therefore, may be that we are living a false life, another person's life, and not our own.

In contrast to this ordinary, outer-directed way of living, I suggest that each one of us has his own personal, inner life story, unique to himself. Each one of us not only has a story that we tell the world outside—our job, our profession—but we have an inner life story that we spend all our lives telling ourselves alone.

The whole idea of an inner life story came to me through reflection upon my own inner life. I recalled the "stories" we told ourselves and acted out as children and began to notice that we might still, as adults, be doing the same thing. I was aware of the current notion of "parent tapes" and "scripts," but I had something deeper—and lifelong—in mind. Our inner story is the content of our most private level of consciousness. It is the actual reason, the final basis of the decisions we make—decisions that are often baffling to others.

We not only *have* an inner life story, we *are* our inner life story, which forms the plot, the outline of our innermost, most private fantasy lives. I cannot prove this to you, except to say that I know myself to have such an inner story, but I am sure that I don't have to prove it anyway—you can prove it to yourself by a moment's reflection. And that may not even be necessary, for by an immediate intuition, most people to whom I have broached this insight have confessed that it is true.

I feel that most of us do not know our inner story very well. Perhaps we did once, when we were small, but years of being told "to grow up," to stop "telling stories," to "be realistic," and the pressures of conformity brought on us by school, military service, work, and the community around us have driven our personal story to the very bottom of our minds. We have a sense of nostalgia when we think of childhood—have you ever wondered why? It is because nostalgia is a sense of recognition of loss; something is gone that once we had. What is that thing we have lost? Our personal story, our dreams, our hopes, our plans for the future, that's what we dimly sense that we have lost, in the bittersweetness of nostalgia. It is our fantasies about what we are going to do that are gone. And that loss leaves us with a haunting, lingering undertone of sadness, which sometimes looms up in the middle of the night when we can't sleep. That upswelling is not of the past and its memories but is the still living inner fantasy that is the real clue to our life—the clue we regularly ignore.

Loneliness, boredom, frustration, a sense of failure, but of what we do not know, all these hurts and more finally arise out of the shunting aside of who we are and want to be in favor of being and doing what other people expect us to be. We hurt, and being mistaken about the source of our hurt, we strike out at other people and them, too. Such is the price of growing up in conformity, in ways pleasing to others and not in growing up by fulfilling our selves. As the medieval theologians said, sin is choosing the unreal over the real.

Decisions and Fantasy

Sometimes it takes a shock, a sudden flash of recognition for us to become aware of important facts about ourselves and the world. Recognizing that we all, even the most stolid of us, have fantasy lives, may serve as that needed shock.

On every side today we hear of mid-life crises, of people suddenly losing interest in their homes, families, and jobs. Or, as one of these people put it, of discovering that we never really were interested in our homes or vocations. Marriages of twenty years begin to fall apart. Foolish behavior threatens the positions men and women have sacrificed to attain. A reasonable question is "why?" Perhaps the insight that we have an inner fantasy life that cries out for attention may provide part of the answer. We may have repressed our innermost dreams and desires for so long that they suddenly rise up and demand attention in middle life. Like a vitamin deficiency, a lack of fantasy and fulfillment may affect one's life as a debilitating disease. Anxiety, depression, irritability, the vague but unshakable feeling that we are unhappy and that there is little to live for, can be the direct result of such depression. No wonder systems of meditation are so popular today! Many of us do feel renewed when we are "given permission," authorized, as it were, by an expert, to just sit and think. Meditation does relieve anxiety, as many scientific tests indicate and hundreds of testimonials certify. But I wonder if meditation is enough? Do we not also want to change our lives? Don't we wish to change from deadened ways of living to more vital ones? I think we do.

Just here decisions must be made. Often decisions are taken that result in broken homes, destroyed jobs—in tasks of reconstructing a new life at a time when age and physical health are more suited to the enjoyment of a life style attained by years of hard work, together. Such decisions are sometimes necessary, of course, but not always. Nor do such results of mid-life crises necessarily give one more happiness. A newly reconstructed life is a happier one only if the person "lucks out" and begins to live in accord with his or her inner fantasies.

A serious consideration of one's inner story and a decision made to develop that story in one's everyday life might preclude drastic changes in middle life, or, at least, make sure that any changes would really be satisfying ones.

For those who are already in middle life and are facing the reassessment of their lives that middle age brings on, there may be some helpful guidelines in the book, *Your Exciting Middle Years,*[6] written by Rachel Conrad Wahlberg and this author.

Perhaps thinking about one's inner story can help the reader find access to that dimension of himself where his own inward fantasy lives. I think that I have said enough about the constructive aspect of personal fantasy to show that I am not recommending simple daydreaming or escape from reality. How can we make life decisions that are meaningful, if we do not take our fantasies into account? The point is not only to get our heads straight, but to get our lives in order and to live in deeper harmony with others as well. A better understanding of our personal desires can lead us to more genuine friendships with others and to a greater appreciation of the world around us. Attention to our fantasies may result in behavior that pleases both us and others.

Long ago, the Roman emperor Marcus Aurelius said, "I, too, am a man and nothing that has to do with mankind is foreign to me." Fantasy, pursued with an active imagination, can lead us to this empathy with others. It takes imagination to feel empathy—imagination and a feeling for the wholeness of life in the world.

Most people who have lived in cities have seen people wandering down the street, talking to themselves. As a young social worker in the Philadelphia slums, I remember being singled out by the alcoholic crazies for their harangues. I stopped to listen once and was asked for money. "What will you do with it?" I asked. "Buy a drink," was the old man's reply. I was so flustered I gave him a half dollar. "Remember, I told you what I would do with it," he told me as he walked away. Here was a man telling a sad story, but at least he had his story straight.

Our first reaction is to avoid such people, to pass by on the other side. We are all too aware of the noisy people. What we do not notice are the silent people who pass us, undoubtedly telling stories as full of pain as those who weave toward the gutter, shouting to themselves. We are even less aware of the many others who sit on park benches like stones. Without imagination, we will never have the human feeling to say to both the noisy and the quiet ones— if only to ourselves—"Hey, what are you doing?" Perhaps if we really ask them, they will tell us, "I'm telling myself a story." If we then respond, "I'm telling myself a story, too," the world might be changed for the better, for them and for us. In that flash of recognition, our common humanity would be established, and some sense of community formed. We would not be able to tell each other the whole story of life, but we could help one another to write the next line.

The Adult Life Cycle

What I am suggesting here is that the hurts and cares of life grow out of ourselves and of our own shortcomings rather than being thrust upon us by others. People who have been sinned against by unfaithful partners, ungrateful children and meddlesome relations may smile cynically and dismiss this idea as nonsense. *Nevertheless, I repeat, the source of our hurts lies inside us.* It is because we are the kind of people we are that other people and circumstances can hurt us. More and more psychologists are writing from this same perspective. Dr. Wayne W. Dyer tells us we have erroneous zones.[7] Dr. Theodore I. Rubin tells us we harm ourselves by the way we handle anger.[8] I'm suggesting that our "erroneous zones" (or areas of unhappiness) and the anger that may poison our lives both arise out of trying to be something we are not (living by a "false script"), and then inwardly demanding that others give up their freedom and play roles, too.

It might be well to point out what psychologists today consider the stages or phases of the adult life cycle. We have become used to his conception of stages of psychological development in children and young people; now we must become accustomed to thinking of adulthood as having its stages of growth, also. As we consider these stages, we will also mention some of the major "hurts" or problems usual in each phase of life.

Briefly, the adult life cycle has these recognizable stages:

Ages 16–22—Leaving the family, moving out in the world on one's own.

Ages 23–28—Reaching out, preparing for one's life's work, establishing a family.

Ages 29–34—Questions and turning points, the first crises of identity and meaning.

Ages 35–43—The mid-life explosion—marital problems may come to a head at this time.

Ages 44–50—Settling down.

Ages 50–on—Maturity, mellowing, the fullness of life.

Life is not easy. After the first four or five years there are probably no unbroken "happy times" in any life. Living is hard because it is serious, the only reality. It is pure sentimentality to think that childhood is carefree and full of joy.

Childhood has many hurts, and adolescence is full of miseries that we forget in adult life, yet we carry their scars for life. No one is in touch with his feelings who doesn't know this.

Sometimes I like to think of my childhood and youth, now that I am middle-aged. "Nostalgia" for the "happy days" of yesterday is a current subject of conversation in America. No doubt we did have more energy, more dash when we were in our teens. But the fact is, we had more fears and perhaps more psychic pain, too. Growing up is a hard job. "Growing pains" cause "stitches" in the side, nervous tremors in the joints, and pimples on the face and chest. Not really knowing what runs the world and what is hogwash causes both pain and anxiety. It's a good thing teenagers are strong and brashly brave, or they would not survive to "grow up."

No, I don't think I'd want to be a teenager again. Cutting my lower wisdom teeth on a troop transport and growing my first whiskers during a war—a war fought mainly by teenagers—dampens my nostalgia.

The Life Cycle

Perhaps it is only as we grow older that we can begin to be honest about our childhood and youth. Childhood is not that unspoiled, happy time that myth and legend make it out to be. If a child's problems are small compared to that of an adult, we must remember that a child is smaller than an adult, too. Many things cause hurts to come into a child's life. A bully at school or a member of the opposite sex for whom one really cares, but who spurns the person, can cause real unhappiness in a child. Perhaps it is a teacher who is overly strict or is not responsive to the child's needs that puts sadness into a child's day. In our day, of course, there are the broken homes that cause much suffering to children as well as to adults. Children worry about things and as they go into their adolescent years, many of their minor hurts become major sources of misery.

As we move through life from childhood to adulthood, we go through some readily recognizable stages of psychological, as well as physical, growth. The psychiatrist, Dr. Erik Erikson, has identified and named some of these stages. We must bear in mind, however, that these developmental phases are not to be identified with age levels or with the physical degree of growth of any individual by hard and fast rules. These are "types" or generalities, and particular individuals can't be forced into molds they don't fit. An 85-year-old person may never have made all these stages or phases successfully, while a 20-year-old person may have completed them all.

The initial identity crisis, according to Erikson, is one of coming to *basic trust versus mistrust*. This challenge arises during the first year of life. The source of its solution lies in the love given by the mother to the child.

The second crisis revolves around *autonomy vs. shame*. Shame grows out of a mistrust of the self. The battle here is fought over the control of the bowels (Freud's anal stage).

If autonomy is achieved (self-control of the bowels), then self-pride develops and one moves on to the struggle for initiative versus guilt. This struggle revolves around the discovery of one's sex organs and means the basic establishment of a sexual identity.

Industry vs. inferiority comes next. Here one secures recognition as a person by making things. Play is vitally important here.

Upon entry into adolescence, the stage of *identity vs. identity diffusion* is reached. Some kind of self-identity, of ego integration must be reached. Many human beings do not adequately master this challenge, due to defects in the establishment of basic trust and self-pride at earlier stages.

Intimacy vs self-absorption comes at the stage of entry into adult life. Here the person must learn how to relate intimately, frankly, openly with another human being. This is a prelude to courtship and marriage. Where intimacy is not reached, the person may remain cold and distant or may make repeated attempts to establish intimacy ("fall in love") and repeatedly fail.

Think back on your teenage years. Those years were a time when you were concerned about the opposite sex and therefore concerned about your appearance. You may have had a problem with pimples on your face or a belief that somehow your hair was too straight or too curly, or not thick enough, or that your eyes were the wrong color or that the shape of your face wasn't attractive. All of these things caused hurt. And, of course, children in their adolescent years can be tremendously cruel to one another. This is the period of time when young people form cliques or groups and run around together. What happens to the child who is rejected and left out? These are the years of dating. What happens when someone doesn't ask you for a date? There are many hurts when you are growing up, and they are not just confined to growing pains and the bewilderment that comes upon one as he grows older and has to face the adult world.

The first stage, then, of the adult life cycle begins around age sixteen, and continues to approximately age twenty-two. None of these stages of life are hard and fixed. Some people enter them earlier and some later. Some people never complete these "life cycles" successfully. But roughly, from about sixteen on we begin to make plans and take steps to leave home.

This is a time when the fledgling flies from the nest. There are many, many occasions for hurt at this time, hurts that we will carry with us for the rest of our lives. There is, first of all, the kind of guilt that one feels when he has to turn his back upon parents and home and all that has protected him up until now, and goes out into the world by himself. It's necessary that children do grow up and go out into the world, but it's hard to justify hurt sometimes, particularly when childhood and youth still draw us back. Many times, too, parents don't make it easy for a child to make this transition from young person to young adult because they keep saying, "Stay awhile, stay back, perhaps that's not right. You're too young to marry. You're too young to consider leaving college," and all the other warnings we remember hearing when we were growing up. This stage of leaving home and setting out on our own is a time of many regrets. It sometimes seems as if we're darned if we do and darned if we don't. No decision is free of criticism by someone.

Part of the problem is establishing our own identity. Erik Erikson sees this as the period when identity is the challenge which the human being faces. Part of the problem can be that we form an identity that is not really ours. This is what I meant earlier by not finding our own inner story. Perhaps we form an identity that is given us by the community around us or by other people who are significant to us or who have power over us. We know that there are some very cruel family situations where a person is told, "You're lazy, you're no good, you're dumb," and other negative judgments that strengthen in the person only a lack of self-worth and negative self-image. There are some people who feel that to establish some sense of identity or adulthood they must engage early in sexual activity or other actions they would rather not do. A young man may not feel he is truly manly unless he shows that manhood perhaps by seducing a girl, or going into the armed forces to show his bravery, or racing a car dangerously. The important thing about expectation and images of self laid on us by other people, whether they are close to us or in the community at large, is that we take on a role in life that misses what we really are and what we really might like to do. Establishing ourselves, going out in the world, can be an occasion of trauma and hurt, just as the birth process itself is one of trauma. The problem of adolescence is greater than that of birth, however, for the blows life gives us at this time can destroy us completely.

Marriage

Reaching out and establishing ourselves as separate from the family, among many classes of North American people, involves marriage at an early age. Here is where so many of the social problems that plague the community and individuals come about. We know that the younger the couple marries the higher the statistical chance that their marriage will end in divorce. Through the years as a pastor and as a professor, I have had many young friends, much younger than I am, and I have seen them go through two marriages and a divorce. There are many things that we do to ourselves simply because we start out in life unprepared. We start out not telling our own story, but doing something to show others that we are truly adult. We are digging our own grave, as it were.

The time of life for leaving home and establishing ourselves, from sixteen to twenty-two, is an exciting time to live, and yet it is a period of time that is full of hurts; hurts that continue to plague us if they are not healed, even later in life.

After age twenty-two, beginning around age twenty-three and running on to twenty-eight (although this is not a set or fixed period of time) we have a second period in life that we might call "reaching out." From twenty-three to twenty-eight will be a time in life that sees most people marry, if they are going to marry. Someone has said that the optimal age for marriage is twenty-five, and by age twenty-five most men and women who are going to marry have done so. This is a period when we reach out and enfold that great world around us into ourselves. Now we establish our own home. Perhaps at first it is only a furnished room, and then a small apartment. Little by little, in our society, as one or perhaps

41

both partners work, they build up their home. By age twenty-eight, all but a very few people in graduate schools have completed their education. Attention can now be directed toward the "nest." The couple buys furniture, appliances, and a small home.

During this period, the first child or even several children will be born. It seems as if the soul and the body of the new family are just reaching out, bringing into itself all sorts of experiences and making strides in the world. This can be a tremendously happy time. In marriages that have a chance of success, the early years are often very happy ones, although difficult, from a financial point of view and in terms of adjustment—psychologically, socially, and sexually. It is not the occurrence of these problems, which are perfectly normal and human, that causes hurts, although they can leave scars. It is such normal problems not adequately dealt with that can lead later to loneliness and frustration, to boredom, and to a host of other ills that plague us in our later years.

Reaching out, a time when the newly emerging person and family spreads itself across the landscape and begins to bring back into the home the riches it gathers there through its work, through its study, through its travel—these can be wonderful years. They can also be times when, some five years into marriage, people find that they are not suited to each other. The couple finds they will not work together. That marriage may then come to an end or enter an unhappy period of cohabitation without true communication and caring for one another.

Once more, because a first marriage fails there is no indication that life will be lived full of hurt and unresolved miseries. Everything depends on how the person takes the experience. Future success in marriage rests on whether the person learns something from the experience and does not create the same problem again. Much depends on whether we forgive the partner we have broken with and whether we have forgiven ourselves. Divorce is not a nice thing, nor a thing to be desired, and yet it is no different from any other human problem. Divorce is certainly no more sinful than to wrong-headedly perpetuate a marriage that is miserable and unfruitful for the partners and for the children. Better to end it reasonably and try to begin anew. Everything depends on whether forgiveness is sought. It is important to clear, as it were, the mechanism of our mind and our soul of all the hurt and the frustration and the anger that can build up when a marriage comes to an end. I have suffered through these periods of time with many people. When finally the legal decree is granted it is often anticlimactic because most of the hurt has been worked through by that time.

Divorce is not new. Divorce is provided for by the very law of Moses in the Old Testament. But in the past thirty-five years, the number of divorces in our society has drastically increased. In 1975 there were more divorces granted in the United States than there were new marriages contracted! More than 35 percent of marriages contracted in America end in divorce within their first ten years. Some lawyers and sociologists predict that the divorce rate will rise over the next few years to 50 percent.

But people continue to marry, usually between the ages of eighteen and twenty-five, in America. Psychologists believe that the choice of a mate made at this time probably is not a fully conscious, mature choice, but one based on unconscious motivations. Later in life, as we become more self-aware and conscious of the realities of life in the world, our choice of partners may seem obviously wrong to us. Thus the great increase in divorces today is indicative of men and women who are searching for their true identity, seeking desperately to live their own story. The answer then, to the problems posed by an increasing divorce rate, rests on waiting until later in life to marry. One needs an adult ego, a fully developed self-identity to enter into a fruitful, long-lasting marriage.

After age twenty-eight, when one has either reached out and established the home that will endure for years to come, or else the first attempt at family building has broken up, we come to a period from age twenty-nine to thirty-four, which we might call a time of questioning and crises. This is a mid-life period although it is not middle age, but a period around the age of thirty that causes people to examine themselves. Gail Sheehy in her book, *Passages, Predictable Crises of Adult Life*,[9] has coined a phrase that I think will grow in popularity because it covers an important event. She says we enter a "Catch 30" situation. In all honesty, I believe I thought more deeply about entering the age of thirty than I did of turning forty!

What does Gail Sheehy mean by "Catch 30"? I think she means that feeling well-known to us from movies and drama, from reading and the jokes that we tell, and from our inner experience if we are fair with our memories of our late twenties and early thirties. This is the feeling that somehow a milestone is passed when we reach the age of thirty. We seem to think that youth is behind us when we are thirty, and we are committed now to aging. We are entering a time of adulthood when there is no chance left for us to be a child again. We recall the slogan of the radical student movement of the sixties that said "Never trust anyone over 30." This is ridiculous, of course, and yet it builds itself around our own feeling of the significance of the thirtieth birthday. These common feelings do tell us something real about the spirit of man, that age thirty has a special meaning, that it marks a turning point in life.

What are some of the problems that hurt us just now? What are some of the turning points that come at age thirty? Many elements are involved here, but the first two areas of life that every human being would point to are those of marriage and occupation.

Advantages of Age

What do the candles on your birthday cake indicate? Simply how many times the sun has set for you. That's all. They don't say how well you function, what jobs you can perform, how healthy you are, or how well you fit into society.

Dr. Robert Kastenbaum, noted geriatrics specialist with the University of Massachusetts and consultant to the U.S. Senate's Special Committee on Aging, believes legal age is an inaccurate measurement. He says, "An individual's calendar age is unreliable and not very useful for many purposes. A person may be sixty-five by the calendar but really much younger, both physically and mentally, than a person of fifty-five." [10]

Dr. James Fozard, clinical psychologist, formerly on the faculty of Harvard Medical School, has this comment: "A quiet revolution is underway. There is a growing awareness that the date an individual was born is not as important as his physical, mental, social, and psychological ages when it comes to his ability to perform. As employers begin to rely more and more on functional age factors, the actual date of birth becomes less decisive." [11]

An older employee has a great deal to offer his company in wisdom, experience, judgment. He usually knows how to make a decision, when to make it, when to speak, when not to, how to counsel. He probably knows how to listen . . . a quality that is rarely developed before middle age.

Our present concept of when a person is middle-aged is subject to change. With the increase in life expectancy and higher health levels as a result of current efforts to retard aging, people may soon be living to age 140 or longer. Then middle age will be placed at seventy. At a time when our nation is faced with shortages of many goods and services, we should be thinking in terms of a person's ability to contribute skills, no matter what his racial, sexual, or chronological statistic.

History provides abundant examples of people who reached their peak of performance after middle age. Verdi composed "Othello" when he was seventy-three. Cervantes wrote *Don Quixote*, when he was well into middle age. Benjamin Franklin invented bifocal lenses when he was in his seventies. A prominent San Francisco pediatrician retired from practice at the age of seventy to take another four years' graduate study in medicine. Now she is working again in an allied field with a full schedule of new patients.

Author of many novels and benefactor to hundreds of human beings, Pearl Buck said on her eightieth birthday, "I am a far more valuable person today than I was fifty years ago or forty years ago, or even ten years ago. I have learned so much since I was seventy! I believe I can honestly say that I have learned more in the last ten years than in any previous decade." [12]

Faculties can't be measured by calendars. There is no inevitable lessening of intelligence or learning capacities after middle age. Studies by the U.S. Department of Health, Education and Welfare show that smart people tend to get smarter as they grow older. The brain is like a muscle. The more you use it, the more it develops. Each one of us has an individuality, a unique fund of wisdom and experience that can be used to benefit society and ourselves. There need be no diminishing of vitality, creativity, and achievement with advancing years.

What can you do to perpetuate your zest for life and your ability to function well? Dr. Kastenbaum suggests we stop celebrating birthdays. He says commemorating our birthdays is the worst kind of conspiracy against ourselves. Our consciousness of the passing of time can be a cause of aging. Years alone can't produce degeneration.

A group of medical specialists and surgeons in the staff

conference at the DeCourcy Clinic in Cincinnati reached the following conclusion: "Anyone who thinks that because he is getting along in years he should experience loss of vigor, debilities, or degenerative disorders is suffering from time neurosis, which may be more effective than physical conditions in producing the effects he fears . . . vigor does not necessarily vary inversely with the average adult age. But belief in the effects of time tends to reduce ambition. Therefore, expectations and endeavors are curtailed. Those who develop a time neurosis subscribe to the prevalent superstition that time is in some way a poison excreting a mysterious cumulative action. The obsession itself may be the cause of definitely premature aging." [13]

At the Age of Thirty

By the age of thirty or thereabouts, we begin to ask ourselves whether we have found the fulfillment in marriage we might reasonably expect. A man or a woman who is working might ask whether or not he/she is climbing the career ladder in a satisfactory way for someone in that profession. If the woman is no longer working or has never worked, she may ask herself if life is passing her by. She may begin to wonder whether she should complete her education and enter the work force, or else find a teaching position or the niche in the business world that she occupied before her children came along. The age of thirty is a time when we begin to see that life isn't endless and that we have to make up our minds and make some effort to begin to build the life that we want to have.

At the age of thirty, if marriages have survived up until now, they may still undergo a strain. It's a period of time when we may feel we're growing older, and either the man or the woman will want to show he/she is still as young as he/she would like to be. They may try to demonstrate this by flirtation with other partners. This can bring a strain on the marriage in itself. More likely than not, where there are these kinds of extramarital affairs, something is wrong in the marriage itself. In fact, these affairs might be indications that the person is attempting, in the wrong way, to deal with the problems of a bad marriage. Many hurts come to the fore when we are near the age of thirty.

The feminist movement has brought to our attention the plight of many women in our society who are precluded from their full rights and privileges, from finding the kind of fulfillment that men supposedly do in business and industry. Around this time, then, we see some women showing their awareness that the feminist movement has something to say to them. Nothing said here is meant to deny the truth found in the charges of the feminist movement. Frankly, feminists are saying something a democratic, Christian person must agree with. But what I want to observe is that not only women have such problems, but men do, too. If a woman is unfulfilled, by being kept at home, away from public life, without contacts, with simply the care of children to take up her time, then the man in that situation who toils to be the bread winner also may be unfulfilled. He may be distorted out of a recognizable human shape himself by such an arrangement.

I would suggest that there is no partnership in which one side of that partnership is denied the full attempt to grow as a human being, that does not, at the same time, cause the same warping of life for the other partner. Long ago historians studying slavery pointed out that the very act of keeping someone or some class of person as a slave deformed the slaveholder and the whole society around him. So if the feminists' charges are true, and I think they are generally true, it is not only women who are living unfulfilled lives in our society, but men as well. Perhaps if women and men in marriage relationships were to look at each other and see this fact, instead of blaming one another or negotiating for their own kinds of freedom or denying it to others, we might all become more human and avoid some hurts in life.

As they approach or reach thirty, people in the professions may find that it is the time for finishing the final training or education needed in our heavily credentialed society. This was my experience as I reached thirty. I decided that I must finish my doctoral program, begun years before. Under the pressure of an increasing family, I had left school to teach for several years without completing the doctorate. I knew that if I was ever to be fully qualified as a university professor, I must finish that doctorate. Besides, I felt this lack of completion as a dangling thread in my life, and I wanted to tack in that loose end. So around the age of thirty I began looking for fellowships and opportunities to take leave from my teaching position and return to graduate school. This is a tremendously difficult and hard experience for anyone. It was doubly hard for me. We found that financially I could not afford to take my family with me to Chicago, to attend graduate school. I was going to have to leave them 900 miles away and be able to visit home only rarely. What a wrenching experience that was!

Leaving the respected and fairly easy position of a college professor in a small town, living at home with my wife and children, and going away to a cold and distant city where I was only an unrespected graduate student, all by myself, was quite a blow! Then there were the difficulties of the extremely hard studies and the difficulties of trying to hitch-hike home to my family. This was not the hardest part, as difficult as the doctoral program was. The most wrenching experience, perhaps one of the most painful experiences in my life, was leaving my family. It was not made any easier by the fact that I left at the end of the summer just six months after my third child, a dear little girl, was born. Looking at that baby in the crib and turning away to get in my car to drive to Chicago was more difficult than climbing

over the side of the troop ship to take part in the Inchon
Invasion in the Korean War. Leaving my children was more
painful. You have a lot more to lose at age thirty than you
do at age seventeen.

Life is like that and at age thirty we may do many painful
things. Surely those people who come to the decision that
their marriages are going nowhere, that they are extremely
unhappy and who break up a relationship in which they
have seven or eight years of their lives invested, must go
through a pain much worse than mine was. I knew that in
some higher sense my pain was all for the best. It would be
better for me and for my family if I could finish my education. To break up a marriage and have to admit defeat is
much worse. I cannot feel superior to such people who have
these experiences though. Today one out of three marriages
ends in this way. I can only feel the hurt that must be theirs
and pray that such people can endure it.

Life is not easy. Whoever told us it was? I cannot buy
much of the popular philosophy that travels around our
country today or much of the popular religious belief that
talks about life as all joy. I feel these outlooks do not fit my
experience. I also feel that such views do not fit the realities
that are taught by Scripture and developed by the great
Christian theologians. Life is not easy; it is full of hurts. Life
has always been full of hurt and always will be. We cannot
escape hurt; we can only learn to roll with hurt's punches and
learn to live with it. What about sin? Those who think that we
can tell ourselves there is no hurt, that we can live trium-
phantly and victoriously all the time, forget Christianity's
teaching on sin. I don't believe that Christianity is masochis-
tic or that it has an evil or negative view of life, but I do feel
that Christianity is realistic. I think whenever we believe that
there is no hurt or that it can be avoided, then we have
committed the heresy of denying original sin.

Original sin tells us that no matter how intelligent we are,
we will sin. It is our nature to be selfish; it is our nature to be

shortsighted; it is our nature to be concerned not about others, but about ourselves and our own feelings. So, in our self-centeredness, we hurt ourselves and others and we hurt God. I think we must face up to sin and to the fact that hurt is a part of life.

I believe that Leibniz, the great eighteenth century philosopher, was right when he said that this is the best of all possible worlds. God made this world and he made it to take into account that man in his freedom would sin and would destroy and warp many things. Yet God ordained that he could bring good out of evil. To deal with hurt is not to deny it, it is to accept hurt when it comes, to overcome hurt. We can only do that by forgiving others, by forgiving ourselves, by living constantly in the forgiveness of hurt, attempting to throw off hurt and forget it. We can only live happily if we are willing to accept difficulty; if we are courageous enough to struggle, even though wounds are possible. Every adult bears scar tissue. We must learn to see scars as part of living and not as some unwarranted accident. God did not promise us a world in which there would not be suffering, but he did promise us that the suffering would be redeemed.

The Mid-life Explosion

After the questions and problems that arise in the early thirties, comes the period of time that we now call the mid-life explosion, beginning about age thirty-five and running to about age forty-three. For a long time, this period of middle life was ignored by most scholars and commentators. Some years ago, I became interested in this period of time because I was approaching forty myself. It was coming very close—I was thirty-nine. And so I began to do research, as is my habit, and I discovered that there was almost nothing in either the medical or psychological literature that treated this period. I did some research and gathered what data there were to be found and produced a book entitled, *Religion After Forty*.[14] Eventually, because many millions of other people were also interested in middle age, several other popular books were written. Later, Rachel Conrad Wahlberg and I produced another book for Word, Inc. entitled *Your Exciting Middle Years*.[15] This went out as a media kit so that people in churches could study the problems that face us in middle life. Now there are many books out on this life period. Perhaps the most famous is the one I mentioned earlier, *Passages: Predictable Crises of Adult Life* by Gail Sheehy.

Statistics gathered by sociologists have caused us to pay more attention to the mid-life explosion of late. Today we are seeing marriages that have survived for twenty years break up suddenly. We are beginning to understand that the middle of life, rather than being a comfortable period (as it might be), can be a very uncomfortable period indeed. In a society that stresses sex and sexual satisfaction so highly, men who are entering middle life, who may feel some decrease in their sexual drive, may begin to panic. The very activity of adultery may grow out of a man's desire to affirm that he is still potent, still a man. We need to face this sexual panic. Such a panic may be true of women as well. Our society, we know, places a great deal of stress upon physical attractiveness and women want to believe that they are not getting older, they're getting better! Of course, women want to be attractive. And of course, it is true that many women are not getting older but they are getting better. Women may be forgiven this anxiety because of the stress that the mass media and their neighbors place upon sexuality, which causes them to wonder if they are still desirable.

I wonder if we realize how much we are manipulated by others when we begin to engage in sexual activities? These sexual expectations can bring a tremendous strain upon a marriage. So widely accepted is this particular strain that there are books calling for open marriage, swinging, and sexual experiments that seem to say such sexual experiences are needed for psychological health. We ought to understand, with compassion, those who wrongly accept this social expectation. For surely these extramarital affairs are the occasion for much hurt, both within and outside the marriage. They are the occasion for causing misery and suffering in the lives of others—for the spouse, the children, the family, and even for society itself.

But it is not only sex that becomes a question during the mid-life explosion. There is also the question of vocation. If, at the age of thirty, we begin to wonder if we are climbing the career ladder in a way that we should be, this is an even sharper question at age forty. Our society defines success in terms of ownership of home and cars, bank accounts and opportunities to travel, clothing, and fame. We might ask ourselves have we really achieved success? Newspapers and magazines tell us about people who have "made it" and we look at the family situation comedies on television and see all that they have and do, then look at ourselves, concluding that we are pretty drab. The mid-life explosion could well grow out of a sense of insecurity as to how well we are doing in the world. If we measure ourselves by the size of our bank accounts instead of by the depths of our spirits (as is the whole message coming to us from this society), a good deal of unhappiness may be in store for all of us at this time of life.

One middle-aged student of mine has written why she signed up for a writing course in her middle life:

> It's the challenge of doing my own thing at 50, to feel that I'm still growing and learning and accomplishing. I believe very strongly that women in their middle years (actually the longest period of their lives) need to feel that life is not meaningless, that you can become most truly yourself at a time when you have less need for dependence on others. For once, you can be free of the roles you assumed all those years and can discover the unique nature of the person

inside you. I've discovered that a part of the person inside me wants to write.

But the mid-life explosion has a deeper significance than the reassessment of our sexuality and finances. There is a sense in which we recognize that more than half of our allotted time on earth is gone. We begin to wonder if we will ever fulfill any of our dreams. Perhaps, here in our dreams or daydreams, in our brooding as we drive our cars, some of that inner story—those real wants and desires that are deep within us—may begin to surface. Such a situation could be healthy. We could begin to see that we ought to be our own person, and we ought not to live, as the psychiatrist Dr. Dyer calls it, in our erroneous zones. We can begin to see that we ought to live our own lives and not the lives that are laid on us by others, whether they be our spouse, our parents, the mass media, or our employers. Then a real crisis may arise. We can have a kind of death panic. We can begin to wonder if there is still room for change, if we can still grow. If this happens, we fail to have faith in God and the common sense for true self-evaluation that we ought to have.

We need to look around more broadly and see, not how little we have accomplished in forty years, but how much it is possible to continue to accomplish in our forties, fifties, sixties, seventies, and even in our eighties. Being a parish pastor has certainly taught me something in this area. I don't think I ever realized, before the last six years of my pastorate in a semi-rural congregation, how alive and young and creative people are in their seventies and eighties. The people who live in the countryside in Ohio have taught me a lot. I worry a good deal less now about how much I have accomplished and can accomplish in my forties, when I see people in their seventies still alive and vibrant and working hard and doing things.

We even have statistical figures from sociologists and economists to show that workers on the job are less accident-prone and accomplish more as they get into their sixties, so that a worker of sixty-five, generally, is less likely to miss days from the job, to hurt himself, to do poor work than a younger person. The older worker is, in short, a very efficient employee. But then our social custom of forced retirement at sixty-five comes along and says that he has to leave the plant or the office. Many of the things we do out of supposed rationality are not very reasonable.

The fact is, although half of life may be gone at forty, half of life still lies before us, and that second half can be far richer in achievement, even in the sense of worldly success, than the first half. After all, our education is over, for the most part. We now know what we are about. Generally, at this time there are not too many changes in career, although it is possible in our rapidly changing society with the freedoms that are ours in North America, to change careers at this time. But even if a change happens, there are many carry-over skills for living now part of a person in his forties that make achievement in a new field more possible than it is for a younger person. Mid-life crisis, as a fear-of-death crisis, may arise out of failure to consider life and the world objectively.

There is a reason for this warping that affects us in our middle life and can also affect older people as well. This is the great youth orientation and worship of youth forced upon us by the mass media and the entertainment industry. There are very few stories, novels, plays, and movies which show us the beauty of middle age and the dignity and achievement of old age. Rather, we are asked to look up to youthful heroes and heroines, to stars who are young or made up look much younger than they really are. It has only been in the last ten years or so that there has been a move away from the extremely glamorous type of person presented to us by films as the ideal type. I've written about this in my book, *Finding a Simpler Life*,[16] finding meaning in our turn to heroes and heroines who are plain, as we are. Today we are beginning to see that one may not look like a Greek god or goddess, but he/she can still be beautiful, attractive, and desirable. One can be plain and still be worthy of respect. Yet that youth orientation is still with us in society. It is really a problem. It's a problem not only for people in older life, but it's a problem for youth, too.

I wonder if we realize just how big a problem, just how much unnecessary hurt, how much surplus suffering is caused by unreal standards in life, such as the worship of youth? We miss, then, seeing all of life as full of possibilities. The unreal standards of beauty and handsomeness I've called "Hollywood beauty" have caused problems for young people, too. I wonder if we know how much misery some girls suffer because certain unrealistic measurements, body types, and facial features are held up to us, again and again, in the mass media, as being what a woman ought to look like? I wonder if we know what it does to men who may not have an hour glass figure and may not be broad across the shoulders and extra tall, to have held up to them the picture of a surfer type as what men ought to look like? All these things, which cause us to question ourselves, can really be the sources of suffering for young people too.

The young person with pimples on his face, who may still be too skinny or too fat, according to the stereotype, can be utterly miserable. The young person who is not wealthy enough to dress in the latest fads and fashions may be awfully miserable because he doesn't meet that social standard of good looks. And these kinds of standards are really hurtful as we grow older. Our hair begins to thin and turn gray, and we begin to find ourselves (supposedly) unattractive. We begin to have a bulge around the middle and our muscles, which may never have been large, have become flabby. Of course, we could exercise and be healthier for it, but we can't exercise ourselves into looking like some Superman or Wonder Woman. Although we like to look at these extremely attractive people, I wonder if we know what

56

we are doing to ourselves by allowing ourselves to inter-
nalize the worship of beauty and of unreal standards of
youth and fitness?

All of these unreal standards of our day strike us with a
terrible force in middle life. We must begin to recognize
that we are getting older. Men see their hair falling out.
Both men and women see it turning gray. Bulges come in
the wrong places. We don't have the wind or energy we
used to have, and wonder if it is just a long slope downhill
from now on.

Perhaps this has affected me, too. I don't think I would be
able to function as a counselor or teacher, and certainly not
as a writer, if I didn't go through all these mistakes and
miseries myself. Being pretty stupid, I haven't had to pre-
tend these miseries. I've felt them, but suffered through
them. I think, to be fair, that I've thrown them off faster
than most. I know, a few years ago, out of no conscious
thought that I wasn't as athletic, as muscular, as courageous
as I once was, I did some foolish things. Perhaps I'll do
them again, because I proved to myself under those foolish
tests of my endurance that I wasn't too old for adventure.
One of those tests I did was to take my twelve-year-old son to
Mexico, to set out on foot with packs and a little water and
food, to go walking through the desert and hillsides of
Mexico, far away from everything. I found that I could do
it. Perhaps unconsciously, I had to prove that I was still a
young man.

Facing Our Mortality

In the universal sense that we all die, we must come to
grips with our mortality and our finitude. We must come to
grips with the fact that death will come to us as it does to all
people. But more than this, the period of settling down
must be a time to come to grips with the particularities, the
peculiarities of our own individual lives. Here is where the

adult life cycle will begin to evaluate itself. Now our story might become clearer, either by way of regret and remorse that we never really lived our story, or by a kind of left-handed benediction that will tell us, as it so often does in God's grace, that despite ourselves we are living out our story, even though we weren't aware we were doing so.

I need to illustrate this for you. It is perfectly possible, in this period of life, to look at yourself with realism and objectivity. You will find, God willing, that you have done the things you wanted to do, and you've done the things you had to do. Our destiny is a combination both of our freedom and of those elements of determinism in our lives over which we have little or no control. Elements of determinism, of course, would be our race and our sex, the period of history into which we were born, the country into which we were born, the kind of parents we had, the kind of educational opportunities made available to us, without any choice on our part. Many other elements such as the state of our health, the state of our intelligence, the state of our emotional strengths—all are givens or elements of determinism. They are part of the way God structures the world. On the other hand, there are limits to freedom. There are the facts that we can think, that we can reflect, or conversely, that we can fail to reflect, we can fail to think, that we can think foolishly or act impulsively. We can make choices that decide between this and that. And this is what I meant by our freedom.

Our destiny, in the final analysis (and we begin to analyze that destiny in this period of life), is the combination of the choices we've made in our freedom and those elements of determinism which occur regardless of the kind of decisions we make from day to day. Such is our destiny, what we wanted to do and what we had to do, mingled together. The illustrations I give of this might be surprising to you.

I think of the great Protestant Reformer, Martin Luther. Luther's father was very important to him, much more than his mother. His father had always felt that he should "take charge" in the world, that he should be a leader of men. He particularly pointed to the law as a way, in that day as in ours, of ascending to a responsible position in the community. Of course, we know that Luther disappointed his father and it seemed as if his father's wishes, which were in some sense a kind of life story which Luther internalized, would never be fulfilled. First, Luther underwent the conversion that led him to a monastery and to a severe form of medieval Catholicism. He became a monk and celibate so that he would never be able to have children and never exercise authority in the secular world in the sense that his story had been told by his father. But interestingly enough, God was able to use that kind of freedom of decision (and even the kinds of determinisms in society that led a man like Luther into celibacy and the priesthood), to work in such a way that his story did come true.

As Luther grew older and underwent the tremendous conversion experience that led him to found Protestantism and become the founder of the Lutheran Church, we find that he left the monastery, establishing the Protestant parsonage, involving himself in the life of the community, even on a national and international scale. He married and had children. As he reached maturity, at this age of settling down, he had achieved all the things his father held out for him and which we can believe were his inner story—to be a leader of people and to be a father of many children, to communicate, as it were, his name and fame to the future, through parenthood.

Luther, as he reached this period of his life, age forty-four and later, was asked for advice. His advice was taken seriously by princes and electors, by senators and judges, by people of all sorts, not only the clergy and Christian lay people. And Luther was a father and husband of note. Such is the way our inner story may work itself out no matter how drastically it may seem we have departed from it.

59

There are many other illustrations in life that we could give. There are the sad cases in which people have developed a negative self-image. They felt they were no good and that they must fail, that they must come to a bad end. Then they went out in life and became very successful. It seems as if their story led them through a series of crises and they ended up just the kind of failure they had predicted and apparently desired for themselves. It is a strange thing. We need to be careful of the story we are telling ourselves, and we certainly need to relate that story to Almighty God and his plan for our lives.

I don't want to give the impression that we needn't pay any attention to our inner story, to our wants and desires, that we shouldn't process our own thinking, our own feelings and pay particular attention to them and to our relationships with other people. Not at all. I do want to suggest that we shouldn't despair, that we may surprise ourselves. Our stories, the meaning of our lives, may be told, may be accomplished, by the grace of God.

The Age of Maturity

After the period of settling down, and an individual reaches the age of fifty, he or she has entered that period we will call maturation—maturity, mellowing. Here, while life is far from over and we are quite capable of all sorts of creativity, new inventions and hard work, still it is a period of time in which we begin to enjoy our labor, to take a new perspective on life. After all, we have lived half a century, we've been able to make some judgments about the world and about life. We shouldn't be so susceptible to fads and vain philosophies, as the Bible calls them, as we once were. A more settled approach to life is ours, as well as a more conservative outlook, although not necessarily in the political and social sense.

A conservative outlook, in a healthy sense of the word is

one of wanting to preserve and conserve those values that have been tried and true—to keep those beliefs, doctrines, ways of living, ethics, laws that have shown themselves to be promotional of human happiness and harmony, to be constructive in life. It is a great benefit of this period of life that sound ideas and values become clearer in our minds. We begin to see that all the idols have feet of clay, that our ideas are mixed. We begin, perhaps, to have judgment, mature judgment, and to choose those things that are good and to let go of those things that are not so good. Our joy now is to find the treasure that comes to us in earthen vessels, that comes to us with feet of clay, and to preserve it.

In this part of life our children are probably grown, or are close to it. We may find ourselves undergoing hurts and challenges from new directions. There may be a sense of aimlessness and loneliness, a sense of purposelessness that can settle over a marriage, for example, when the children leave home. You know, for so many of our years in marriage and raising a family, everything is determined by the needs and demands of the children. This is not a bad thing, of course, but it simply means that the mother "bird" is so busy getting worms for her "birds," teaching them how to fly, that she has little time to think about her own needs and desires. And now, suddenly, they are all gone. The nest is empty. A great depression can settle over people at this stage and great strain set in upon the marriage. This is a time when hypochondria, a worry over health, over imaginary aches and pains, gives more meaning to life and helps fill up the time. Such self-indulgence can become a great stumbling block for us. Concern over bodily functions is true of both men and women. Now alcoholism can become a problem. Drinking, or drinking more than is good for us, can hold itself out as a way to fill up empty hours. This needs to be guarded against.

From my own experience as a pastor of a Florida church, ministering to a large number of retired persons, I can testify that the drinking of alcoholic beverages is a more difficult thing to deal with in older people than in young people. Now there is a great empty stretch of time. Perhaps we've not prepared ourselves for this period of life. Perhaps our vocation is all we have; there are no avocations or hobbies; there are no interests outside ourselves. Perhaps we have not worked in the church and don't have vital interests in large issues like the overseas missions of the church, or its social mission, the work with the poor, with the dispossessed. There may be no meaning to things. Here is where the misuse of alcohol, barbituates, and amphetamines can enter in. We need to be aware of this as a possible source of problems. We need also to know that a heart full of interests, healthy interests, will not have room for these kinds of interests—negative interests—at all.

Beyond fifty, we would not place any great limits upon this period of maturation. Surely it encompasses the period to age sixty-five. Here people work with regularity. There is no good reason why people shouldn't work beyond sixty-five, except for the fact there is need to make room for others in the work force. After sixty-five, we might think of ourselves as entering a plateau, a holding pattern during the retirement years. These could be happy and fulfilling years as they are for many, or they can be lonely and frustrated years. Many hopes are battered, and many dreams don't come true. There are many hurts that come to people during retirement.

What are some of these hurts that come after the age of sixty-five? The hurts in this period are many, just as the possible blessings are many. First there are hurts that are connected with our children.

By this time our children have reached maturity themselves. They will be out in the world, making a living, married in most cases. Now we may receive hurts from observing or perhaps from becoming part of their lives, and seeing them make their own mistakes. Some of these hurts are quite genuine hurts, that can be understood. Others are the results of misunderstandings. None of us likes to think that our children are imperfect, but we are certainly setting ourselves up for hurts because of our lack of realism if we expect any human being to live without making a mistake. In our day, parents of this age often have to stand by and support their children as they go through divorce actions. This can hurt. If our own divorces hurt us, surely the divorces of our children can hurt as much or more. We will have to stand by and see them as they make their first tentative attempts at parenthood, as they make their own mistakes with their children, as we made our mistakes.

There's a hurt, too, that comes when bad health becomes a part of our experience. We want to point out that to be over sixty-five is not synonymous with bad health. But we do know that as the aging process increases, as we go into our seventh, eighth and ninth decades, the processes and systems of the body do have problems. We should not be surprised that bad health comes to us in later life from time to time. Hurt can come from this, but perhaps even more hurt comes when we witness the bad health of a loved one. Here is where the husband may be very unhappy as he observes his wife with a disease, or becoming a bed patient as a result of an injury. A wife might feel hurt as her husband shows the results of the strain of a life of working and suffers a heart attack. Here also emotional problems can emerge. There is the very strain of retirement itself. The changed situation in life might cause one to unfairly judge that he is worthless because he no longer works. Feeling useless really does hurt us! And the feeling is so undeserved.

Here, too, in this last major constructive area of life, sixty-five and past, many hurts can come if our life story has never been attained. Regret can be severe and profound, not in the sense of foxhole religion or fleeing to God when there is nowhere else to flee, but in the sense of turning to that which we should have turned to all along. We may find that we need faith and trust in God. The person who missed the middle-life crisis, or who did not respond to the middle-life crisis effectively, may in fact have to respond here and now in this period of life.

Enough has been said about the stages of the adult life cycle to show that we do have some sense of how a normal human life progresses through adulthood. I believe that we have also pointed out the major kinds of hurts and problems that may come to us in our period of history, in our kind of society. We are not saying that all of these problems, or even a majority of them, will be yours, but we do say, without threat of contradiction, that problems will come in your life, as they do in mine and in everyone's. Hurt is a part of life. The goodness and graciousness of life that comes from God is marred by human sinfulness. This sinfulness is more than simply the sum of individual human choices and acts, but is a rebellion against God, deep as the spirit in man. All considerations of life and its meaning must take this sin into account. We can only point here to the One who can heal—to the cross of Jesus Christ and his atoning blood. We can only affirm that this makes sense, is understandable against the backdrop of sinfulness, our original sin which is rebellion against God.

The way beyond hurt and through hurt, the way to happiness, is through realism, not through belief in a fairy tale that nothing is really wrong with the world. We cannot talk or think our troubles away. The hurts of life are real, as real as the pain we feel in our flesh and the upset and unhappiness we feel in our minds. The hurts of life are as real as the nails that nailed Jesus to the cross, and the answers, the solutions, the helps, for those hurts are as real as the One who offered his life as a ransom for ours.

Selfishness As a
Style of Life

Selfishness As a Style of Life

Tom Wolfe, the satirical social commentator who helped found "the new journalism" writing style, recently analyzed current religious trends in America for *New York* magazine.[1] Wolfe, who is as perceptive as he is humorous, declares that ours is a generation which places great emphasis on "Me"—all of us want "to talk about me" and few of us want to listen to others.

Wolfe's is an acute observation. We do live in a very "me" centered society. Most of the popular religious and psychological movements of our times stress the "me" much more than the "our" side of human experience. When we say that we want "to communicate," we often mean we want to tell others about "me." This is as true of charismatic services and confessions of sins in conversion-oriented Christian worship services as it is of primal scream therapy sessions. "Hey, look at me. Listen to me," seems to be our national refrain.

There is nothing wrong with valuing the self, of course. As Jesus put it so clearly, "So whatever you wish that men would do to you, do so to them; for this is the law and the prophets" (Matt. 7:12). St. Augustine, too, wrote of the Christian's duty toward himself saying that a proper self-love was not only permissible, but healthy and the foundation of love of others.

Immanuel Kant, the great eighteenth-century German philosopher, put the value of the person as person at the center of moral life, writing in his *Prolegomena to Any Future Metaphysics*,[2] that every human being is an end in himself and never a means to an end. A person has dignity, an intrinsic value, on which no price can be set. "Skill and diligence in work have a market price; wit, lively imagination, and humor have a fancy price, but fidelity to promises and kindness based on principle (not instinct) have an intrinsic worth." [3]

Kant sees human dignity as resting on human autonomy, in that persons share in the making of universal law by their moral decisions. He restated the Golden Rule as: "Act only on that maxim through which you can at the same time will that it becomes a universal law." [4] Or: "Do unto others as you would have them do unto you."

And there's the rub. We are willing, all too willing today, to talk about ourselves and to claim our rights to self-development, but we aren't too strongly motivated to give the other fellow his chance to talk about himself and to realize his growth. Insofar as we behave this way, we are utterly selfish, and we also show an underlying hurt or pain in our spirits. We might say that our pain expands to fill whatever space is available. Anyone who has had a toothache or an upset stomach realizes the truth of this observation. Pain tends to push aside all other awareness in favor of itself. The person who is distressed, frustrated, depressed, or fearful cannot appreciate love or recognize the needs of other people, except in a fragmentary way. Epicurus was surely right about that upset stomach! It is said that friendship doubles our joy and divides our sorrow, but it is also true that internal confusion and hurt chokes off and divides our joy and doubles our grief, by narrowing our horizons of awareness. We find ourselves today cut off from others by the moral and psychic pain that also fuels all the "let's talk about me" religions and psychologies enjoying such great success around us.

Loneliness

Ultimately, our problem today is loneliness in the midst of other people's company. We are together, but only in the physical sense. Loneliness, of course, is never a question of place or time. There are no lonely places, only lonely people. And we are not made lonely by others—we choose it for ourselves.

Loneliness may be the result of pain, but of pain misunderstood, rather than of simple pain. Pain, whether physical or mental, can teach us something of life, if we will let it. We can learn from pain that our bodies and those of others are dense, heavy objects. When they collide with one another, pain results. Anyone who has played touch football knows that. More than this, the human spirit has "density," too. When our spirits collide with that of another, in confrontation, anger, rebuke, there is also pain.

Loneliness grows out of pain—not only the experience of pain, but the fear of it. Perhaps it is this fear that hurts us most, since it turns our spirit inward in an endless cycle. Because we are hurt by others, we are afraid of relations with others; because we are afraid, we therefore hurt others by our coldness and rejection. Then, in desperation, out of fear that we will lose all there is to life, we reach out in some unwise way for fulfillment—or at least satisfaction—and only succeed in hurting someone else. And so it goes, the cycle of loneliness turns and turns.

Loneliness then, one of the major forms of hurt for both younger and older people in our society, is a hurt of the spirit. It is not a description of how many people are present at one point in space and time.

If loneliness is a way of life not dependent upon our

surroundings, then it is clear that loneliness springs up from within ourselves. People are quite lonely in large cities, perhaps more lonely than in quiet, rural places, since trust is lacking between people thrown together in urban areas. Go to Bug House Square in Chicago, or the Bowery in New York City, and see for yourself the loneliness of the crowd. "Myself is hell, which way I fly, is hell," says Lucifer in Milton's *Paradise Lost*. If we find we cannot empathize with our spouse or children, then the problem is within us and within them, not in the space between us and them. The empty miles of barren tundra that march to the top of the world across the face of Canada and Alaska is as close to its Creator as Toronto and Miami Beach. Such places are not lonely, but loneliness is a human quality that grows out of human hurt. It is the result of either an active or a passive rejection of others. There are no lonely places, only lonely people.

The hurt within us that causes loneliness to grow is the apprehension that we do not care for anyone else or that others do not care for us. Loneliness, whether it begins with us or with someone else, grows out of a fault in caring. It is the result of undervaluing ourselves, undervaluing others, or of being undervalued by others. Paradoxically, loneliness is a cooperative experience, just as exploitation is. To suffer from loneliness, we must fail to value and to care about our self and others.

We cannot be rejected fully, without rejecting ourselves. Loneliness is thus the selfishness of despair. We can see this syndrome of despair in Jack.

Some years ago I was invited to give a lecture at a small midwestern college. At that time I met several faculty members and students whom I was to come to know as friends from that day to this. One of these new friends was a student named Jack.

Jack was, and is, a handsome young man with many talents. He was infected with the competitive spirit, had

70

high ideals, and believed in his future. Jack was oriented toward success. During his college career he held most of the student government offices and even made an attempt at a civic elective office. In this first campaign he, not unnaturally, failed.

After college Jack began graduate studies in another state but found most interesting his work for a rising political figure there. Soon he left graduate school and ran for office again. Once more he failed, although he came close to defeating his older opponent. Then he went to work in the state government. When election time rolled around again, he ran for office once more. This time Jack came within a few hundred votes of winning, but once again he failed.

The toll these campaigns and defeats took on Jack was enormous. The psychic pain he received from what he interpreted as rejection was very great. But in time, he recovered enough to return to graduate school. Now he is living a kind of simple, drop-out life. The routine of everyday work doesn't seem to appeal to him. He has moved far away from his friends, home, and family now. If he has any realistic ambitions for the future, they are hard to discern. He did complete his graduate work.

Jack is not the hippie type. He loves the good life of luxury. It is easy to see that Jack equates happiness with success and success with public acclaim. Considering the emphasis on just those elements in our society, it is not surprising that Jack has internalized such values. What is tragic is that Jack isn't truly happy as he is. Instead, since Jack has been unsuccessful, he has locked himself into a sphere of loneliness. He will never come out as long as he fears more rejection by the world.

"Nobody wants me; nobody likes me; I'm gonna eat some worms!" Loneliness like this can easily lead to depression. Sometimes we are so close to people we can't see a serious depression coming. Once, one of my church members committed suicide. Only a short time before our families

71

had gone on a picnic together. Neither the man's wife, nor his children, nor his pastor guessed the lonely despair he was feeling. Only his death made us aware of the problem.

Depression also leads to aggressive behavior toward others, or to quieter attempts on one's own life. A seminarian's wife tried to commit suicide twice in one year, as a way of announcing her feelings of being left out, of being lonely at theological school. Loneliness hurts.

Recently a husband returned home to find a note on the table which read: "Took Mom to emergency room at hospital. Joe."

The husband was upset, to be sure, but more than upset, for Joe was only thirteen years old and couldn't drive a car. When the man reached the hospital, he found that several of Joe's school friends, ages thirteen and fourteen, had been visiting him when they were disturbed by choking noises from the mother's bedroom. The woman was an alcoholic, totally drunk, and beginning to strangle on her own vomit. Somehow, the young people got her into the car, drove the car to the hospital, and saved her life.

There are thousands of drinking housewives in this country who are actual or potential alcoholics. Why do they drink—usually secretly? Not because they are happy and content, but because they feel trapped by marriage, frustrated, and bored. Such secret alcoholics have also retreated into a private sphere of loneliness, where they drink to deaden the pain of their despair.

There are many kinds of people in the world, but I have come to believe that most of us fall into two basic types, the active and the passive. Some of us respond to life's challenges, opportunities, rebuffs, and hurts by withdrawing unto ourselves, while others respond by reaching out and taking action. Loneliness can, therefore, be dealt with by both withdrawal and over-activity. To "run around" too much may be as sure a sign of loneliness as staying at home.

To attempt to lose ourselves in the world by constant movement is sign and seal of our inward hurt, insecurity, and loneliness. As an active person, I have had reason to recognize this problem in myself.

I left home when I became seventeen. I wanted to be on my own. I thought I could go my own way and find my own friends. I felt no need for family or commitments. Other people have had the same experience, I know, but I was, in truth, the very model of the rebellious, independence-seeking adolescent. I can recall, ringing in the back of my mind, my grandmother's quotation from the Bible: "For none of us liveth to himself, and no man dieth to himself. For whether we live, we live unto the Lord; and whether we die, we die unto the Lord: whether we live therefore, or die, we are the Lord's" (Rom. 14:7, 8, KJV).

In time, I discovered that these words are true and that I was wrong. After dropping out of high school, joining the Marines, fighting in Korea, I ended up in the university. One day I read the famous words of John Donne: "No man is an island, entire of itself; every man is a piece of the continent, a part of the main. . . ."

Although I have always been an independent, lone wolf type, I now know the Bible and John Donne are right. We *are* parts of one another and we must learn to live together, not by means of subjugation or for profit, but by cooperation and comradeship.

This insight is shared by many, but practiced by few. Therein lies a large part of our hurt.

A *Phenomenology of Being Hurt*

We often say things like "your actions really hurt me," or "I was hurt by the outcome of the election." At other times we say, "I fell off the ladder and hurt myself." Or "I slammed by finger in the car door and it certainly hurts."

73

We use the word *hurt* interchangeably, both for a physical hurt and for bruised feelings. We can be hurt in our emotions, how we feel about ourselves and others. Hurt refers, too, to damages and pain connected with our physical bodies. This is perfectly proper usage, and it is not a confusion to use the word, "hurt" or "pain," to refer both to the emotional and to the physical sides of life. It is imperative that we use common words in both these ways because there is no radical division between the emotional life, the mental life, and the physical life. I am a total human being; I am one person. I have a body and a mind and emotions, all together. Nevertheless, we must ask: What is the nature of hurt when it is physical? What is the nature of hurt when it is psychological? Is a hurt in the soul of the same order as a hurt on the bottom of the foot? Let's see if we can bring some clarity to our use of the word "hurt."

First of all, consider the ways in which we use the word *hurt* and the kind of human experiences that we have, and others have, to which a word like hurt or pain, or suffering and cognate words apply. We will find that all such occasions have one characteristic in common. The characteristic element is that we are shocked, we are surprised, we are taken aback. We are moved to ask ourselves, if only in some mental shorthand, "*What* is happening to me?" "*Why* is this happening to me?" Or "Can this be happening to me?"

I think my reference to shock and surprise might be a little clearer if you would think about the last time you twisted your ankle, or hit your finger with the hammer, and suffered pain. The first thing you asked yourself or that you felt was —"Can this be happening to me?" Or, "*This* is happening to me!" It's a shock! There is a surprise. And there's a sense of incongruity. We may even say it aloud, "This can't be happening to *me!*"

A good indication of the truth of this last assertion might be found in someone who is held up by a mugger and is struck by his pistol. The person may say, "This can't be happening to me!" It can happen to someone else perhaps. It can happen in a book or movie, but it can't happen to me. We are incredulous, we are frankly shocked. We are surprised that such an event can happen to us.

From this it follows that one of the characteristics of the experience of being hurt is that it calls our self-worth into question. We undergo a crisis of the meaning of ourselves when we are hurt. Sometimes when a hurt is physical and not awfully painful, and where the most severe hurt is to our ego, or pride, we may express this in some way, trying to deflect this loss of self-esteem. For example, we may say, "I'm such a klutz," when we trip and fall. But there is a sense in which the whole meaning of ourselves is called in question when we are hurt. Believe me, this is doubly true when it is a question of a wound, or something that we did not invite—something that we have dreaded, something that suddenly happened to us.

It is well-known that in the psychology of battle, a soldier would be unable to function very long if he did not somehow believe that death and injuries and wounds will come to others, but they will not come to him. This kind of denial of death is frequently met in human beings. Freud suggested it is one of the great untruths or self-deceptions by which men live. Yet it is absolutely indispensable, in some real sense, for those who find themselves having to undergo the hazards of conflict. This is true of the policeman and the fireman, I'm sure, as well as of the soldier.

As we look at hurt, even in its physical manifestations, twisting an ankle, striking a finger, being wounded in battle, there is that shock, that surprise, that immediate drop in self-esteem, that denial—"This can't be happening to me." We can already see that hurt is an emotional as well as a physical event from the very inception of the experience. It is not a question of hurt happening to the physical body and then being translated into an emotional stress; rather, the physical and the emotional reaction are one and the same, and they occur together.

A related element in the experience of being hurt is the sense of violation. There is a sense of *lese majesty*, of a crime against the dignity of the person. Of course, when an injury is self-inflicted, even by accident, there is a sense of guilt or self-blame for having offended our own dignity. Then there is a double bind, both of guilt and lack of self-esteem. We experience a drop in self-worth, as well as a sense of being violated, in this case, by our own shortcomings.

Obviously, when we are wounded or attacked by others, when we might be struck by someone, there is a real sense that our life space and the dignity and the sacredness of our body, of our meaning as persons, has been violated. This is true of psychological hurt as well as of physical hurt. Let us say someone snubs us in the old-fashioned sense of that word. Someone "high-hats" us, simply turns a cold shoulder and ignores us as if we weren't there. As far as they're concerned, we are nothing. We are reduced from a person, who is the center of dignity and meaning, who demands attention, to something not worth noticing. We are simply snubbed with noses turned up. When this happens, we are immediately shocked, surprised, and we feel a drop in self-esteem. Perhaps we shouldn't, but we do. Our dignity has been violated. We immediately think, *He can't do that to me!* The thought that someone could treat us in such a dehumanizing way shocks and almost paralyzes us. A psychological hurt like this is as damaging—and can be even more damaging—than a physical injury. Being hurt turns loose all kinds of negative thoughts in our minds, and feelings of anger, rage, and frustration may overwhelm us.

A graduate student of mine was once bested in an argument with another student and walked away hurt and depressed. His hurt soon turned to rage. The student came to my office and choked out his problem, his face engorged with blood, red and fiery. Suddenly he struck the cinder block wall with his fist. His knuckles were cut and bleeding, but he grinned sheepishly and walked out. He felt better. That's the kind of anger psychological hurt can generate.

The best way to demonstrate how we hurt is to recount some true stories. Here are a series of anecdotes based on actual pastoral counseling experiences. These are normal everyday people who attend churches like yours and work in offices and factories like everyone else. These are not stories of terrible sinners. Troubled people surround us on every side, and we may be hurting, in our own way, as badly as these people hurt.

Intimations of Mortality

Edna Black was fortyish, stylish, and well-educated. Edna's husband was a prominent, wealthy professional. Her children were bright and ranged from high school age to one already married. A casual acquaintance would have said that Edna had everything. She did, but what she had included an unresolved development of her sense of self. A crisis arose when Edna was suddenly struck by a series of deaths among her family and friends. She was overwhelmed by the finality of death. All at once the secure world she had built up was exposed as tottering on the brink of extinction. Like the rich man in the parable, her barns were revealed as poor guardians of her ultimate worth. Edna faced the despair of ultimate meaninglessness. The situation was worsened by the fact that one of the deaths that affected Edna was a suicide.

Edna mourned and groped for something stable in a world where everything dies. She was fortunate in being a part of the church. In the Christian community, she found solace and the strength to begin life again. Edna still hurts, but not so badly that she cannot seek to turn back and build up parts of her personality she had previously ignored.

William is an athletic man in his middle forties. Prominent in his community and successful in his profession, "Willie" is usually outgoing and full of fun. But a few years ago, Willie found himself in a severe depression, brought on by labor unrest, strikes, and court settlements on the job front and precipitated by the death of his father.

Willie had always loved to travel to exotic places. Now, he had no taste for travel. He had usually enjoyed his work, even when it meant constant courtroom battles with feuding labor unions. Now, the constant pressure irritated him and left him physically fatigued. All the sweet juices of life had run out. Happily, Willie had many Christian friends. They closed in around him and gave him support. Gradually Willie pulled out of his depression. Since his friends involved him in their activities, he discovered that he had a flair for acting and took part in a church play. Willie still has the job pressures, but his depression is gone. A hurt that is shared is a greatly diminished hurt.

The Malcolms are a conventional mid-American family. Their life style is comfortable and without money worries since they own a profitable business. The Malcolms often fly to Florida or California for the sun or fishing. Theirs was a happy, generous family. Then the roof fell in. In an improbable sequence of events, three deaths and several severe injuries struck the Malcolms in a short period of time. Such was the severity of these experiences that no one could fault this family for becoming depressed. The Malcolms had been hurt, badly.

Yet, marvelously, this family weathered its sorrow and continued to function well. In every moment of pain these people turned to the church and their Christian friends. The community of faith helped them to live through events that we all must face, even if not in such a concentrated form.

Shattered Relationships

George is in his late twenties and has just entered his second marriage. His first marriage proved an unhappy one and was broken by unfaithfulness on the part of the wife. George and his new wife are very happy and want nothing so much as to have custody of the two children from George's first marriage. They want to build a family very badly, but don't seem to be able to do so.

The courts have ruled that George cannot have custody of his children, but only visiting rights. George would only be normal if he were disturbed by this situation. He was upset by it, but he has accepted what is and is making the best of it. George plans to have his children when they become old enough to make the legal decision to come to him. Meanwhile, he goes on with his life.

Sometimes we are not grateful for everyday things, like the happiness of having our own children with us. George knows what a blessing that is and also knows the hurt that comes from broken relationships.

The stories of how we hurt in our normal, everyday lives are many. For example, we might not think it an occasion for a great deal of pain when adult people in their thirties want to get married. But there is the case of Clarence and Alice. They are either divorced or separated from their respective spouses. Both of them have children by their previous marriages. They are living together now and have been for some time, but they are not so much a part of the new wave of moral thinking that they feel comfortable with this arrangement. Indeed, they want to get married. They aren't the "swinging singles" types. They are adults who want to settle down.

One might ask, then, what's the problem? And the answer is, they can't get married. Alice is divorced now and she has two children in her custody. She found her first husband to be a good provider, but utterly boring and too old to be a good father to her children. There was no companionship and in the last year of her marriage she began to run around with other men. Alice felt very badly about that; she knew she couldn't continue without tearing down her entire life. She met Clarence who, at the time, was separated and the new relationship sparked immediately and seemed to be worthwhile. It was so worthwhile that she asked her husband for a divorce and Clarence pressed his wife for one also. Clarence and Alice even moved to another town and there they settled in together, sure that they would soon be free and able to marry each other. That wasn't to be. Clarence's wife fought the divorce for months on end and she used the fact of his cohabitation with Alice as an argument against him. Recently, Clarence's only child, a son, was taken away from him by the courts and given to a foster family. That was a terrible blow to Clarence and Alice. Here is a couple who wants to marry and build a family, but can't.

This whole business of marriage, divorce, separation, and adultery in our time is the great middle ground of most of the hurts and problems for the average person. Take the case of Vonda. She's in her forties, divorced, and has one child. Her marriage was extremely difficult. She had both a domineering mother-in-law and a husband who treated her brutally. Vonda had one or more nervous breakdowns during the years she was married. She has since been institutionalized, having already been previously confined before her divorce was final. Most recently she suffered another round of depression that put her in the state mental hospital where her condition deteriorated. She attempted suicide. When she was restrained because of this attempt, she broke away from her guards and tried again. Fortunately, she only injured herself.

Vonda has been released and lives alone, under medication, but her problems are magnified by the fact that her former husband now has complete custody of the child. She is allowed to see her daughter only a few hours a week. Vonda does not want this situation to continue and is continually disturbed about the child custody arrangements. There is a great deal of suffering here and it is not only the suffering that comes from her mental illness.

Sometimes, in the very course of the day, a family—just like one near you, around the block, or in the next pew to you on Sunday—can become pretty violent and far-out, all in the course of suffering the hurts of life. Consider the case of Norman and Margaret.

This young couple is around twenty-five years old. Norman is a veteran, now in graduate school. Margaret is a young mother who is not happy with her husband's success at college and graduate school, but rather has grown more and more depressed. She became so depressed that she attempted suicide. This attempt was hushed up so effectively that many of the people of the community—a close community around the graduate school—didn't even know about it. Nevertheless, Norman's academic work suffered severely. He was therefore forced into deciding two momentous questions—whether to commit his wife to a mental hospital, and whether to give up his graduate studies and his future goals. All of these things are laid upon perfectly normal human beings and are part of the hurts of our time. Norman has become aware of the excitement he feels in graduate school, he loves learning, and he is going to have to make this hard decision soon.

One might almost build a profile of all the stages of life from the various hurts that can and do occur to people. Consider Dick and Anne. This young couple is around twenty-six years old; he is a professional man with an advanced degree. Anne left college after only two years when she become pregnant with Dick's child. They married then and have had two other children since. Outwardly, they were pretty well-adjusted. But recently Anne had another baby and this was not a sign of their adjustment, but of the contrary. It appears that this child was not fathered by Dick, but by another man whom Anne "befriended." The couple lived in a small town and a tremendous uproar arose because of this situation. So great was the uproar that Dick and Anne had to move away. Dick's attitude toward living was simply to let everything go by easily, to just move sleepily along. He had loafed through college and his professional life, and apparently had loafed at home in the bargain! So far, their problems are not yet resolved, but they are still together and are trying to build a new life for themselves in a new location.

But after many a season and many a year, sometimes the marriage dies. Take the case of Walter and Clara. This couple is in their late thirties and have been married for about fifteen years. Both are well educated. They have studied both in this country and abroad and are very sophisticated in art, music, and drama. But they are somewhat immature in self-control and social relations. Clara once left her husband and three children and lived for a time in an apartment, saying that she wanted to show her feminine independence. Later, she became involved with the law in some minor infractions and was convicted. More recently, Clara and Walter have legally separated and are planning a divorce. Walter is no abused saint; he drinks too much and he seems permanently depressed. Given to flitting from one social gathering to another, he makes a habit of starting projects he doesn't finish. Whether either one of these separations was by mutual consent, or was the action of the wife alone, we cannot tell. Now Walter and Clara live in two different towns and they share the children between them. There is a tremendous amount of hurt in this situation. It shows itself in psychic depression and the children are upset over this state of affairs.

Sometimes marriages don't break up when they might just as well do so. Consider "Don Juan and the Ice Queen." In their late forties, this couple have advanced educational degrees and are quite distinguished. Their achievements in the academic world and in the professional world are very much in contrast to their emotional development. They are simply immature in the way they act. She is extremely cold to him and vocally aggressive to him and in her relationships with others. He is easy-going, smiles a lot, and apparently doesn't think it's necessary to do anything to help his marriage. Their children are intelligent. The couple is separated, but this is not the first time. We don't know how this problem will resolve itself, since little effort has been made by the participants to solve the problem. One friend reports that they are tremendously happy living alone. Perhaps there are some marriages simply unable to survive.

What's wrong with these people? What pains are they feeling? Why do they hurt? What hurts them? Who hurts them? Who are they hurting—to act in these ways? What is the answer—if any—to their problems? It is much too easy to offer standard religious answers designed to fit everybody and nobody. These people are members of churches; they aren't atheists; they aren't ignorant; they are among the people who have it "made" in our society. They are not liberal, by and large, but belong to conservative social groups. Something is amiss in their lives! One fact stands out clearly when we discuss them: There are no innocent or no guilty parties involved in marital problems. There are only very troubled people, which includes not only the husband and wife, but children and, many times, friends and extended families as well. To help these people solve their problems, we must find some way to remove the pain they are feeling, to give them relief from the stress and the pressure under which they live. We have far more than a question of right and wrong, but a question of healing. These people must change because change for them would be healing. The big questions are how will they change, and in what direction will they move?

How Do We Hurt?

Asking how we hurt in our society today may seem a silly question. Either we are immediately aware of the fact that many of us do hurt in many ways—or else we are completely oblivious of the fact that there is suffering in life and we may wonder at the question. But if we are serious we can see that there are many occasions for psychological as well as spiritual hurt and suffering in our society. No matter how well off we may be, there are occasions for hurt. Irritants do not go away, regardless of our external circumstances. I've made a list of some ways in which the average person in the average family might hurt. This is not a list of severe problems, or of families that are disintegrating, but a survey of an average family. (See the chart on page 85.)

The first way that we might be hurting is in the realm of nostalgia. Nostalgia is oriented toward the past. Nostalgia is a feeling of regret or sweet sadness about a supposedly better past. Everything looks better from a distance in time and space. It is true that we may have been happier in the past. If we are athletically inclined, we can look back on a younger period when we were healthier and stronger and see that we were happier then. On the whole, however, nostalgia is ill-founded. The past simply takes on a patina, a sheen of happiness that it didn't have at the time. In any event, even in the best regulated and the most successful of lives, nostalgia can cause a good deal of hurt. It is a way in which we tie up the present by chaining it to the past.

A Brief Chart Showing
WHERE WE HURT

On Part of the Self	On Part of Others
Nostalgia	
Regret	Gossip
Guilt	Prejudice
	Communications Blocks
Anxiety	Secrets
Stress	
Hopelessness	
Meaninglessness	Ill-will
Aimlessness	Dislike
Grief	Jealousy
Anger	Envy
Hypochondria	Anger
Ill health	Carelessness
Stasis (No growth)	Laziness
Laziness	
Immaturity	Blame
Jealousy	
Envy	Unforgiveness
	Stress
Fear of Death	Pressure
Ill feelings	Disrespect
Reticence	Taunting
	Ingratitude
Depression	Foolishness
Poor Self-image	Alcohol Problems
Lack of Caring	Drug/Medicine Problems
	Infidelity
Alcohol Abuse	Failure to Grow
Drug/Medicine Abuse	Immaturity
Infidelity	Faithlessness
No Faith (Lack of Trust in God)	
No Forgiveness	

Secondly, we may hurt as individuals or families by feelings of guilt. Of course, guilt over something we have done that we ought not to have done is hurtful, but it isn't a bad thing. It is the voice of God—the voice of conscience—trying to point out to us that we ought to change, and to seek redemption and amendment of life. But guilt, over something we *have* done, ought not to be overindulged. When guilt is wallowed in and savored as a kind of sickly sweet poison, it can kill the spirit and eventually the body, too.

Guilt also may be falsely felt. We may suffer guilt over things we haven't done, or we can feel guilt over things that we think we did, but didn't really do. It is also possible to feel guilt over things we thought we should have done, but didn't do. That may sound confusing, and it is, but we can suffer from misplaced guilt. This can happen to a sensible person, well-educated, spiritually acute, in an average family. This guilt hurts, nonetheless.

Guilt—both the real guilt for which we should ask forgiveness and put behind us, and imaginary guilt—can be felt as sorrow. A sense of dejection, a sense of sadness, may be experienced. Some of the ancient commentators even called this one of the seven deadly sins. Sorrow certainly does make us hurt. We will look more closely at the seven deadly sins in a moment.

Anxiety

If guilt and nostalgia tie the present to the past, chaining life up, then a third type of feeling chains the present to the future and is also a cop-out. This feeling is anxiety over the future. We often think when we are having a good time at a party or a Christmas celebration, "Perhaps we won't be together like this next Christmas." You can fill in the blanks. "Perhaps we won't be together next Thanksgiving,"

86

or the next birthday, or on some other occasion. In short, we rob the present and the near future as well, of all joy or happiness by thinking sad thoughts about the far distant future. No one has any control over that distant future, so it is senseless to do this. Nevertheless, anxiety is a feeling few of us are able to handle well. And anxiety hurts.

Anxiety may be concerned with an object. For example, we may be anxious about our job, our marriage, our children, our investments, and other real areas of life. Or anxiety can come without an object. Anxiety that does not have an object is an imaginary anxiety, a false anxiety. It forms the basis for neuroses or emotional problems. Anxiety hurts, unfortunately, even when it has no real object, but is anxiety over anxiety itself.

Recent studies have shown that anxiety is a very real component of the successful man or woman in our society. Scientists have divided people into "Type A" and "Type B" people, using the presence of anxiety, drive, and stress in the individual as the measurement for typing him/her.

"Type A" people are stress-prone, achievement-oriented. They are hostile to others but suppress their feelings. Highly competitive, the Type A personality feels constantly pressured for time. Such Type A's are excellent candidates for heart attacks.

"Type B" people are easy-going, express their feelings freely. They are not holding back feelings about others nor are they consciously trying to out perform other people. The Type B personality takes his time and still gets the job done. A Type B is unlikely to have a heart attack.

The Type B is living within the present, without being controlled by the past or future. Type B's have their anxiety under control.

We need to be clear about anxiety. Anxiety is both a psychological and a philosophical concept. All anxiety is not the result of emotional problems or mental illness.

Some anxiety is normal—and even necessary for efficient living. The problem arises when anxiety increases in degree and begins to control one's life.

Basically, anxiety is a painful or apprehensive uneasiness of mind over an impending or anticipated ill. To be apprehensive about something real, something we should be preparing for, is a good thing. As Jesus said in Luke 14:

> For which of you, desiring to build a tower, does not first sit down and count the cost, whether he has enough to complete it? Otherwise, when he has laid a foundation, and is not able to finish, all who see it begin to mock him, saying, "This man began to build and was not able to finish." Or what king going to encounter another king in war, will not sit down first and take counsel whether he is able with ten thousand to meet him who comes against him with twenty thousand? And if not, while the other is yet a great way off, he sends an embassy and asks terms of peace (Luke 14:28–32).

The late theologian, Paul Tillich, defined two kinds of "normal" anxiety experienced by sensitive, intelligent people:

Ontological anxiety—the apprehension and uneasiness, the fear based on the ultimate fact that people are finite, mortal and must one day die. And,

Existential anxiety—the disturbances and fears that befall us in the course of everyday living, such as wars, injuries, failure, and disappointments.

We must bear in mind that anxiety is only abnormal when it is extreme in degree—to the point of incapacitating us—or else when the source of our anxiety is imaginary. Anxiety that keeps us aware of the perils of the real world around us is uncomfortable, perhaps, but it is not a hurt. In fact, we would be hurt if we lacked this normal sensitivity to threats and challenges.

The present, of course, can be chained up within itself, without much regard to the past or the future, to produce another way that we can hurt ourselves. I'm referring here to the sense of meaninglessness or aimlessness that some-times pervades our lives. It is the feeling that our lives are not going anywhere, or that they are not of any real signifi-cance to ourselves or to anyone else. Such meaninglessness may be the result of depression, either physiological or psychological in origin. Or it may be the beginning stage of a depressive state growing out of an event in our lives that we can't handle. The sense of meaninglessness and aim-lessness may be felt as boredom. We need to be aware that such negative feelings can be the beginning of emotional disorder or of mental illness. It hurts us to feel that our lives don't mean anything.

Depression is another category, and we will talk about it again, although not in the clinical sense. Such intense depression is an illness and needs to be treated by a physi-cian. We are thinking here about temporary depression, which we all have from time to time. This may grow out of fatigue. Temporary depression can occur because we have worn ourselves out and don't have the psychic energy to cope with the normal problems of living.

Temporary depression may also come from shock or grief. A loss of a loved one can put us in a temporary depression. This grieving process, which we know to be perfectly natural and necessary, may be experienced over the loss of a job, a child's leaving home, failing grades in school, a bad report at work, or a bad investment, as well as at the death of a loved one. An automobile accident could be the occasion for a temporary depression. When depres-sion is not of a physical or psychological origin, other than the ones named here, there is need for medical help. But a temporary depression is equally painful, although not long-lasting and serious. Sickness, grief, loss, sorrow over the death of a loved one, a severe illness in the family, the break-up of a friendship or love affair, the loss of a job, a child's leaving home, trouble with children or your mar-riage, all are experienced as grief, loss, sorrow. The grief process that takes place at a death also may occur as a result of these other events, such as a divorce. Grieving must come following a loss, and one experiences it or else denies his feelings, which can be psychologically damaging. It is better to go through the grief process and come out on the other side determined to continue living your life. No one could deny that this process is real and that it hurts, even as it cleanses the spirit.

Alcoholism and Drug Abuse

The next category of experience that can be the occasion of much hurt in life is overindulgence in drink. Alcoholism is a widespread problem in our culture. Or hurt may come from drug abuse or the misuse of either legal or illegal drugs. We know that alcoholism is on the rise today. There was a 26 percent increase in the use of alcoholic beverages just in the decade, 1960–1970, and alcohol abuse has been increasing since 1970. Either as an escape from boredom or to give a sense of adventure in life, the use of alcohol by women at home is on the rise. The alcoholic housewife is a common phenomenon today. There is also the use, increasingly over the past five years, of alcohol among high school and college age young people. This is a surprising development in view of the widespread use of marijuana in the schools. But it is true that beer, wine, and liquor are very much the "in" thing among young people today.

Other kinds of hurts that this overindulgence of the self might cause are adultery or fornication, separations, fights, and problems in the families and divorces. These are not the only reasons for divorce, but they are some of the major ones. A great deal of hurt occurs in this same area when we see families breaking up and fights developing over the custody of children. Custody fights sometimes occur because one person is trying to make sure the other person doesn't get custody of the children. This is a serious hurt based on selfishness.

Whenever someone in the family is abusing prescription drugs or using illegal drugs such as heroin or cocaine, we are no longer speaking about an everyday hurt. This is a crisis situation, but it is increasing in frequency in our culture. Drug abuse is almost an everyday problem in our time.

Ill health is another factor that immediately comes to mind when we begin thinking about where we hurt in our everyday lives. Real or imagined ill health probably causes as much sorrow as anything in the world. Illness comes by chance, or by the laws of probability, to all of us at some time in our lives. Not the problem of ill health or a serious disease, but how we respond to it, how we take it, is at issue. I've known people with the most severe kinds of illnesses, who have suffered a good deal of pain, and yet they remain cheerful, alert, and optimistic about life. Other people, with lesser disabilities, become negative and sour on life. So it isn't just having ill health from time to time, or even constantly, but how we respond that determines whether illness really hurts us or not.

Imaginary ill health or exaggerated ill health causes most of the hurts a person feels or a family suffers. There are those of us who *do* enjoy ill health. This is a way of getting attention, a way of making sure that someone is securely tied to us. If people think we are ill they won't leave us, we think. Such hypochondria is a form of pure selfishness. It shows we don't really trust ourselves or feel that we are worth very much, without ill health to make people like us and pay attention to us. Such activity does hurt. The family is never sure, of course, if one is really sick or not. In some cases people may suspect that a person isn't sick, but they don't want to say it. At other times, families are not aware that a great deal of ill health is "put on," so to speak, and isn't really serious. So ill health—real or imagined—can be and is a very large source of hurt to everyday people today.

Debts and the kind of financial strain that come from an undisciplined life style, particularly from a lack of financial discipline, can cause us hurt. It remains true, even in this day when one out of every three marriages ends in divorce within ten years, that financial problems are the number one cause of problems in marriages. If we strap ourselves with debts, if we are constantly anxious, even panicky about how we are going to meet the obligations we have, we can see that this will cause hurt and mental suffering in life. Irresponsibility is troublesome for everyone in the family.

Gossip is definitely a source of hurt for a person and a family. I'm speaking now of gossip that is essentially untrue, although it may have kernels of fact interwoven with a great deal of speculation. Gossip occurs when someone simply takes out his feelings of superiority or hostility against someone else by spinning stories about him. Such gossips may not know or care that a person's reputation is vital to his mental happiness. Yet they thoughtlessly or deliberately tear down a person's possibility of happiness with their words.

Secrets also cause hurt to persons and can cause continuing trouble in families. I have never been able to understand this style of life, but I see it frequently as I counsel people and visit in their homes. This or that family member knows something that he is keeping from another family member. The problem with secrets is that they do eventually come out, or at least there is always the possibility that they will come out. Such a life style causes much mental anguish in the person who is keeping the secret and doesn't want it known. It may also cause anguish to the person who discovers the secret and is shocked by it. I don't know if we realize how this matter of keeping secrets really destroys love relationships.

Associated with secrets is lying. Lying is like keeping

secrets, only it works in a different way. Whereas a secret is kept by silence (or supposed silence), a lie covers up something or pretends something by making up a story that such and such is true. But, again, a lie is something that eventually comes to light. At least a lie has the potential of being exposed. Such a situation may cause mental suffering, anguish, hurt in those who are telling the lie or keeping the lie going, and hurt in the person who eventually discovers the lie. "Oh, what a tangled web we weave, when first we practice to deceive." The web usually trips us up.

Jealousy and envy, which are sometimes associated with gossip as the cause of gossip, are great sources of hurt in families and individuals. Jealousy is the feeling that someone has something we would like, either the same thing or something just like it. Envy is the feeling that one thinks one deserves money, or a person's love, or a certain item of merchandise more than the person who actually owns it. Envy causes many problems in life. Out of jealousy and envy stem hostility, anger, and hurtful behavior in thought, word, and deed.

Anxiety over death and panic over our mortality are causes of hurt and suffering in our own lives and families. Some of us seem to be motivated by a death anxiety or a death wish. This anxiety over mortality, not being able to come to grips with the reality that life is bounded by birth and death, can cause much suffering. Our suffering can translate itself into problems for others as well. The anxiety over death may be at the root of our unsocial habits and bad feelings that cause us to hurt ourselves and to hurt others.

We all talk about communications problems today but rarely do we understand them. Communications may not be the problem. We may hurt other people by communicating quite clearly that we dislike them. We may also communicate harmful information to them. But there are some genuine communication problems. Some communication problems arise because of shyness on our part or on the part of others, or because of an inability to relate to that other person fully.

Often we are unable to really talk to a person quite close to us. We're not talking about failure to talk to those we don't know well, but failure to really communicate with someone close to us, a child, a spouse, a parent, a brother or sister. Though we feel we should be able to talk to these people, yet we cannot. This causes a great deal of pain for us and them, and for other people who know about it, even when we cannot give this condition a name. I would call it reserve and see its origin in an inner shame over the way we have treated or thought about a person, or a failure to accept him as a full adult with the same dignity as ourselves. It can, of course, be something that was triggered by the other person as well. They may have hurt us badly, whether they know it or not. Whether this was deliberate or not, we may not be able to communicate well with that person in the future.

A situation like this can only be overcome when bad feelings are brought out and processed, looked at and forgotten, when we forgive each other. Then we will be able to talk to one another as equals again.

We often talk about laziness. Perhaps we feel somewhat lazy ourselves. I do not mean the natural fatigue that sets in from time to time in all of us, nor the inability to get started on a project. Laziness is almost an illness in which one is unable or unwilling to do anything and lets everything slide. This kind of laziness is called shiftlessness and is a hurtful thing. It causes much hurt to people who may be depending upon us. There is the old saying, "Work doesn't trouble me at all, I can sit down and look at it all day long." This is all too true for many of us. Some people are unable to do things for themselves and can use our help, yet we will simply sit and watch people's helplessness because we aren't willing to become involved. Laziness may seem comfortable and a form of contentment, but basically, it is not. If laziness does not have a physical or emotional basis, it probably grows out of a low self-image. It arises from the sense of not caring much for the self—a lack of belief in our own powers. While there are "work-a-holics" who aren't happy, when we stir ourselves and do things we are happier, with a more optimistic outlook upon life.

Ingratitude is a problem we feel within our own minds and hearts. Ingratitude is a sense that someone—a relative, a friend, a spouse or a child—has exploited us, has taken advantage of us. Someone has taken the gifts we are willing to give and does not care about us at all after they have received these benefits. Ingratitude has sharp teeth, indeed. There is a sense of being violated when we feel exploited by others. Lending someone something and then being avoided so the question of repayment won't come up, can be quite hurtful. It is hurtful to the person who has borrowed from us, too. Shakespeare was right when he said, "Neither a borrower, nor a lender be." If it is at all possible, we should do our borrowing and lending through institutions, like banks and savings associations, and not get into deals with our family and friends. It is almost certain that problems will arise out of borrowing and lending among friends and relatives. I've seen this happen over and over again.

Ingratitude may be on our part, too. We feel a lack of gratefulness to others who have been good to us and these feelings say something to us about ourselves. Our ego is so big, so grossly extended, that we are egocentric and feel we have no reason to be thankful to those who help us. This is a hurt, too.

I would think that the average family's hurts, outside of ill health and financial problems, could be summed up in problems with their children. While this is certainly not the worst generation ever born, we have seen many problems arise between parents and children in the last twenty years.

When we look at all the ways we can hurt as human beings and families, it becomes clear that sin causes hurt.

What hurts us are those things we do to escape boredom, to escape frustration, to assert ourselves against other people and over against the world. We feel that we need more in life than mere survival or security. Our passions must be expressed. We must have adventure and experience joy. Such feelings would be fine if we didn't feel that we can have adventure only by running athwart other people's rights or breaking the conventions or laws of society. Much glee comes from breaking rules. The problem with such glee is that it is soon turned into unhappiness.

If, out of years of counseling people, I had to make a judgment, I would say that most hurt comes out of selfishness, instead of sensuality. Selfishness has its rise most often in a low self-image, in low self-esteem, in a feeling of narrowness so severe we don't feel able to share with other people, to be open with them. The person who is selfish is quite unhappy. Our self-image grows out of our upbringing. Something in the way we were treated as children, in the way, not just our parents, but our peers, our playmates, treated us, causes us to feel that there is something wrong with us as we naturally stand. We feel we are not capable, full, mature individuals. Such low self-esteem can make us quiet and reticent. It can make us stay in a corner and not seek to achieve anything. But people deal with low self-esteem and lack of self-love in another way—and that is by self-assertion. Self-assertion may take the form of all sorts of crimes, as well as just simply being difficult to live with.

Self-assertiveness is one of the clearest forms of low self-image. It can lead to criminal conduct and is seen in the juvenile delinquent. Not long ago, a fine Christian woman, who is director of the probation department of our local juvenile court, gave a presentation describing the characteristics of the juvenile delinquents with whom she works every day.

Basically, there are three characteristics that hold true for most juvenile delinquents. These are:

1. They generally come from broken homes.
2. They generally have a low self-image, low self-esteem.
3. These young people are forced to bear burdens that they are incapable of bearing, when they are still quite young.

The results of these three factors is that young people become unable to cooperate with other people and so they act in unsociable ways. These youngsters have no real sense of belonging to the community or the school group of which they are forced to be a part. Very soon, then, they will break away from the family, leave home, leave the community, leave school, and have a very low view of education and of the entertainment and other activities in which other young people engage.

The juvenile delinquents with whom this lady deals generally come from broken homes. These are homes broken by divorce, separation, family arguments, and fights. They may be one-parent homes. There is a deep sense of insecurity involved in a broken home situation for a young person, of course. The child may feel that if he were really any good his father would have stayed at home. Or he may feel that if he were really worthwhile his mother would not stay out at night and come home drunk. These are the conditions under which many young people who come to the courts have been reared. In one case, a young person came into the court and proved to be the last of seven children in one family, all of whom had become involved in problem behavior. Some of these children were in the reformatory. This kind of situation makes us feel that juvenile delinquency and crime may not be the individual's fault alone.

Low self-image, low self-esteem, or lack of respect for the self is translated, by these young people, into lack of respect for other people. After all, if one feels badly about himself and cannot respect himself, then there is no way to respect others. Even if such a person may feel that other people have a stronger sense of their worth, and deserve it, he will attack that person out of envy or jealousy. It's a circular, almost hopeless situation.

The carrying of burdens that young people are too young to bear is something we don't take seriously enough. Years ago it was the rule that young children worked. They worked in the fields with their families on the farms, and do so even to this day. Formerly there was exploitation of child labor in heavy industry, in the textile mills, and in the clothing industry. Such work kept those children from having a childhood or from getting an education. These were burdens too heavy for young children to bear. There are photos taken at the turn of the century that show small children, ages seven, eight, and nine, standing at the great textile machinery, oiling and tying off the coils of thread. We can see the defeated look on their faces, and we can know what it means to be burdened down with cares too heavy for one's strength.

Sometimes, in our day, the kind of burden a young person is not ready to bear takes a different form. It may be the responsibility for baby-sitting for other children, when one is only a child himself. Or perhaps it is being the only responsible person in a home because the father has deserted and the mother is out working. The child may have to feed and diaper the baby, cook for the other children and himself, and try to clothe them and send them off to school. This kind of strain, even in the teenage years, is too much for a young person to bear alone.

On top of the strain of being a substitute mother or father, the child may have the problem of constant exposure to people who are drinking, taking drugs, engaging in illicit sex, (and these may be their own parents), or having to learn about things that most people don't learn about until they are adults. How can we wonder then, that these young people's lives are distorted? That they are not able to be a part of the school and the community like other young people with a decent upbringing is beyond their control.

None of us would deny that a person who has been exposed to these hurts is damaged. We can understand the behavior that brings these young people to the court, even when we deplore it.

One of the comments that the probation officer made was that she has never seen a juvenile delinquent who was interested in sports or music. These young people were excluded, either by lack of opportunity, money, and lack of interest by their family, from involvement in athletics and music in school. They are not in music which requires discipline and financial help, in plays or in any of the other school activities such as Junior Achievement, available in the public school system. We need to recall this when problems arise in our own families with our children. Are we interested in them? Are we interested in their school? Are we interested in trying to make it possible for them to take part in the opportunities open to them through the school and other community agencies in our day?

Why Do We Hurt?

3

Why Do We Hurt?

For a long time American religion has stressed the love of God so heavily and the possibilities of forgiveness so loudly that we now have several generations of believers unaware that God's love is no more real than God's wrath against sin. Forgiveness, while always possible, is not easy or a light thing for God. What Dietrich Bonhoeffer called "cheap grace" has flourished among us. But grace is never cheap. The grace of forgiveness cost God a great deal. It took the death of Christ to bring God's grace to bear upon us. And grace, when experienced in forgiveness, does not erase the consequences of sin in the world. God forgets and forgives, but the evil we have done remains. We often hurt because we forget this truth.

Many things can be overlooked in life, but overlooked only to our harm. Ignoring the reality and hurtfulness of sin is one of these things. We may wink at God's wrath, but it does not go away. Rather, God's wrath resides in our unconscious selves, and works harm to us, in that we refuse to acknowledge it and seek to have it washed away in forgiveness.

Why, Where, When, Who and How Do We Hurt?

A young man of high intelligence suddenly drops out of school. Capable of an "A" average, he comes home on a weekend and "goes to pieces." His parents, unable to control him, take him to a private psychiatric hospital. What's wrong?

Looking more closely at the young man's problem (we will call him Hans), we find that Hans' mother has a history of mental problems. The family is extremely well off, with access to travel, sports, books, plays, and education. Religion plays a large part in the family's life. Yet something at the center of their lives seems unglued and flaps wildly in the gentlest emotional breeze. Why?

On closer examination, we see a group of people at odds with themselves. These are lonely people. The wife seeks "woman's liberation." The husband seeks career success. The children are left to seek their own way. In their failure, these people are exactly like millions of the rest of us. A family of people with clear identities and a sense of self and place never emerges. The glue of filial loyalty and commitment never sets and their love is shallow. Hans and his family are a parable that tells the story of millions of people today.

When we ask what hurts us, the only answer is *people*. Having a plain face or being clumsy doesn't hurt us. People hurt us when they laugh at our plain faces and say cruel things about our athletic ability. Making a "C" or "D" on our school work doesn't really hurt us. It is only a means to learning. But classmates and brothers and sisters, who call us "dumb," truly do hurt us. People hurt us. Not people in China or Africa, but people close by. People who eat at the same breakfast table, or who sit next to us in class or at the next desk at work are the occasions of our hurt.

Who hurts us? This is easy to answer. "Who" is a general

term—people who are close to us; people we would like to like us, whose good opinion we would like to have and who deny us that gift.

How do we hurt? We hurt through rejection and mockery, through mindless, thoughtless cruelty. Most people, from kindergarten through retirement, including us, operate on the assumption that we can only gain if someone else loses. We can only be secure if someone else is insecure. Only if someone else is unhappy can we be happy.

In our own insecurity, unhappiness and lust to win, we step on the feelings of others, and in turn are stepped on ourselves. Our cruel, corrupt, competitive, highly individualistic society is not unlike the food chain in the ocean, where the little fish is eaten by the large fish, and that fish is eaten by a larger fish, and so on up the ladder.

If people were little fish all would be well. But fish have no emotional feelings and people do.

We hurt in what the Bible calls our heart, in our self-image, in our vision of ourselves and of our worth as persons. You need not be a psychologist or sociologist to investigate this. There is no need to visit a prison or a hospital for the disturbed. You need only visit a playground or a public school classroom. Children are, in many ways, as cruel or more cruel, than grown-ups. Children have fewer inhibitions and less awareness of laws and customs. They can express openly what their parents disguise as jokes or hide in snubs or "strategies." For the cruelty of children is learned—not "natural." It is learned in their homes, not on the streets. The hurts we regularly do to one another are only reinforced by the mores of the street, the classroom, and the playground.

When we hurt depends on who we are with and other circumstances. We can be hurt—or begin hurting—any time, any place. We can be hurt in church as well as on the football field, in the family room as readily as in the locker room. When we hurt is completely relative.

The Frantic Search for Happiness

We are all creatures of moods. We pass from modes of consciousness which are calm, to "jitters," to depression, to "normalcy" again. There is a tide in the psychic affairs of men, yet beyond this emotional cycle there is, in many of us, an anxiety that pushes us on toward a frantic search for happiness. In our society, this quest generally is translated into a search for material security, for money, and for things. Such a search is never-ending, of course, for the amount of money and the kinds of things we search for keep increasing. The answer to the question, "How much does a person need?" is "Enough to be satisfied." But we are never satisfied.

The Roads to Madness

An experienced psychiatrist once told me, "Madness is a state of being desperately unhappy." I've never forgotten his words. While there are undoubtedly many roads to madness, unhappiness with one's self, one's family, and one's situation in life seems an open and familiar one to thousands of people.

This book makes no pretense at psychiatric expertise, and this chapter is not a scientific description of madness. It is, however, a very real picture of the maddening life styles that we meet every day in our relationships with people.

Madness may be defined as a sense of the loss of control over our own lives. It is a state in which we feel we are at the mercy of unconscious forces, or of forces outside ourselves. Since our highly complex lives leave us all feeling somewhat controlled by large economic and social forces beyond our power to influence, there is truth in the popular observation that all of us, today, are a little mad. Social commentators who point to the roots of madness in our general society-wide sense of frustration and powerlessness have a real point.

But individual madness, or a life style that looks and feels like madness is something else again. For the person slipping away ("going crazy"), there is first of all, an intuitive sense that there is a gap between what one actually is and really can do in the world and what one thinks he wants to do and be. "Going crazy" is the process of discovering this inner conflict and of feeling helpless to overcome it. Here, too, actually slipping away into madness is but an extension, an extreme state of the moral confusion that characterizes all of us as human beings.

Paul already noted this inner conflict in Romans 7:18, 19: ". . . I can will what is right [Paul says], but I cannot do it. For I do not do the good I want, but the evil I do not want is what I do."

Paul was writing about sin, of course, but sin, as the deep root of alienation, of separation of the human being from God and of person from person, is at the root of madness, just as it is at the bottom of our unhappiness.

Paul is clearly stating what many of us feel, that there is an estrangement, an alienation between those feelings and actions that promote life and the expressions of those feelings and actions in such a way that human happiness is harmed, not helped.

This is a classic description of what Transactional Analysis calls an "I'm not O.K., you're not O.K." position. Everything is poisoned, nothing can go right, for everything we or anyone else may say or do is already judged negatively before the action starts. "Damned if you do, damned if you don't," the popular proverb has it.

Another name for such a situation is "the double bind." "The double bind" is a crude but descriptive name for one of the most common—and most destructive—relationships that can be forged between human beings. This is a genuinely "no win" position to take in life. When a wife holds this view of her husband, or the husband thinks in this way about his wife, unhappiness is bound to result for everyone, including the children. But far more seriously, we ought to recognize that the person who plays such a negative "game" holds this attitude toward himself or herself. Such a person is sometimes recognizable even to laymen around him. A person who constantly acts in this fashion is popularly called "a loser." He has already judged himself and found himself wanting. What that person sorely needs is a sense of God's forgiveness and acceptance, but it is difficult to get him to recognize the freely offered forgiveness that is the root of the Christian faith.

It may seem silly to say that the answer to madness is forgiveness, but I seriously make that claim. Perhaps it is too late to heal one who is lost in madness, but the experienced offer and acceptance of forgiveness can help a person leave the road that leads to madness. This is true because only forgiveness, experienced and accepted, can overcome the depths of despair and self-accusation that underlie human unhappiness. The opposite of unhappiness is not happiness—it is forgiveness, just as the opposite of happiness is not unhappiness, but first of all, unforgiven sin.

Speaking of God's reaction to the fall of humanity into original sin, St. Augustine observed: "God did not take back all he had imparted to his nature, but something he took and something he left, that there might remain enough to be sensible of the loss of what was taken. And this very sensibility to pain is evidence of the good which has been taken away and the good which has been left." The following stories, taken from a pastor's counseling sessions, illustrate Augustine's insight—pain is both the sign of sin and the evidence of the good God still preserves for us.

Lori, age nineteen, came to our third session in tears. She wept pitifully, confessing, "I'm so lonely that I don't know what to do. I just want someone to love me."

Subsequent sessions with Lori and several conversations with her mother revealed a deeply pathological family relationship. Lori's parents had been separated since she was about ten and she lived with her mother who was very neurotic herself.

Such a background produced in Lori an inner life of which she was almost totally unaware. This inner life was one in which she had a deep-seated need to punish herself, had a low self-image, and held for herself standards impossible for her to reach.

Lori outwardly maintained that she wanted to marry a wealthy and successful professional such as an M.D., a brilliant attorney, and so on. But she was not in a position to do this and probably would never be in such a position in view of her educational and social station. Thus, even though she outwardly professed to want happiness, marriage, social prestige, she was nevertheless living under the direction of her inner life—an inner life which compelled her to fail by setting impossible goals and thus reinforcing her feelings of low self-worth and need for punishment by the certain failure to attain these impossible goals.

Harry, age forty-two, was suicidal. His first marriage had collapsed. His second marriage, to a beautiful girl much younger than himself, also collapsed. Feeling that there was nothing to live for any longer, he alternately cried, shouted, cursed, and whined during our first interview.

Harry was unable to give love, except in the kind of way that made others feel obligated to love him in return, whether or not they really wanted to. Sooner or later, those about Harry grew tired of his attempts at manipulating others into loving him and refused to associate with him. This included his two wives. Thus, Harry's deliberate attempt to insure his being loved only left him feeling more lonely and unloved than ever.

He was living out an inner life in which he felt that the world owed him a loving. Thus, he saw no need to become loving and lovable in return. All that was needed to set things right was for the world to recognize its moral obligation to love him. And if the world failed to fulfill its moral obligation, Harry would see that it did by whining, attempting to manipulate others, making himself appear the victim of injustice, or any one of a thousand other ways he had stored in his neurotic arsenal.

At heart he was a small child who believed everything should come to him with little or no effort on his part. Harry's inner life was, in reality, the life of a child. He was trying to be an adult while emotionally he was still a child. Though he professed adult needs, his demands were really those of a child. His outer life appeared adult-like, but his inner life was that of a child.

Sandi, age twenty-one was hospitalized. In the past she had attempted suicide. During our first interview she rambled from one subject to another. Subsequent interviews with Sandi, several conversations with Sandi's mother, and the chance to observe the interaction between Sandi and her mother revealed a pathological family relationship, with Sandi in the middle.

The effect of this unhealthy family relationship was most marked in Sandi, causing her to alternate between two poles. She desperately wanted to be herself, but years of unhealthy motherly influence would not allow her to be herself. This ambivalence finally became too much for her and she developed some severe emotional problems leading to her suicide attempts.

In reality, Sandi was living out her inner life. Since her mother had surrounded her with numerous "thou shalts," "thou shalt nots," "oughts," and "shoulds," she found it impossible to disobey the voice of her mother. Consequently, Sandi always ended up living out her inner life, which was really her mother's wishes, not hers. It was this civil war, won by her inner life, that caused her to be hospitalized.

Louis Dupré, writing in *The Christian Century* on "The Religious Meaning of Mental Suffering," [1] speaks of mental illness as a picture of the human condition to which religion must speak. The disturbed person is only "ourselves, writ out in larger letters." Indeed, ". . . the salvation which religion promises presupposes an unsatisfactory state of being that must be remedied."

Seen from this perspective, we may wonder if unhappiness is not a universal condition of mankind apart from the healing salvation of God. As Dupré says, ". . . the mentally ill are often more in touch with their real selves than are many well-adjusted persons." Dupré means, of course, that well-rounded, well-adjusted people may be only superficially well. They may be denying the strong forces of the unconscious, turning a blind eye to dead relationships with others and in general, play-acting their way through life. Looking at insanity from this angle, Dupré and others remind us that genius and saint may be quite related to the mad. "Perhaps this experience of the terror of endlessness occurs in heightened form in men of achievement and in the ill," Dupré remarks, quoting William F. Lynch.

Whatever we may think of this analysis, it is clear that religion has always been concerned with healing. The very word "salvus" from which we get our word, "save," means "to heal." Modern theology stresses that salvation is healing and that all actual healing is part of Christ's redemptive process.

Madness comes upon us when the world we inhabit falls apart. Man does not have an environment, as an animal does. Rather, he has a world. Man's world is more than a physical place, it includes—and is partially created by—his world-view, his point of view or outlook. In our world we find largely what we expect to find. We miss those elements of the real world that we are not looking for. If we think everyone is against us, it should not be surprising that we can find evidence to back up our point of view.

The following demonstrates that our distorting or warping of the real world is, unfortunately, perfectly normal. We see a reflected image of our inward values when we look upon

111

the face of the enemy or the form of the beloved. The field of literature is our record of human folly.

Wendy is in her early forties. She is divorced and has one child, an eleven-year-old daughter. Wendy's marriage was difficult. She had both a domineering mother-in-law and a husband who treated her harshly. Wendy had one or more "nervous breakdowns" and was hospitalized both before and after her divorce. Most recently, she suffered another round of depression that put her in the mental hospital. Wendy is home now, but the courts have restricted the amount of time she can spend with her daughter. There is real concern on the part of the social worker for the child's safety. The child also has frankly said that she doesn't want to be with her mother. Wendy is disturbed over this, but she attributes her problem to a conspiracy between her husband and all the lawyers, judges, psychologists, and doctors in town. She cannot focus on her part in the situation. Until she recognizes her role in the affair, she won't be healed.

Wendy's story is drawn directly from life. If you are interested in a book full of such true experiences, you may want to read Otto Friedrich's *Going Crazy, An Inquiry into Madness in Our Time.*[2]

Against these "warps" of reality, we cannot truthfully present an ideal picture of the real world. No one of us is completely adjusted. Everyone of us is somehow neurotic, somehow maladjusted. It seems that our individual maladjustments tend to cancel each other out when we relate ourselves to others. Nevertheless, we should recall that God wishes no one to be unhappy. An old proverb says, "Gladness of the heart is the life of man, and the joyfulness of a man prolongeth his days." And even the pagan philosopher, Epictetus declared: ". . . You were not born to be depressed and unhappy."

Depression

We commonly call a state of chronic unhappiness "depression." This is as much a part of our everyday language as it is of medical terminology. There is little doubt that everyone is depressed at one time or another in his life. It seems to be as much a part of life to be depressed occasionally as it is to have a cold occasionally. It's also clear that something might be wrong with us if we have a cold all the time, or are susceptible to lung disorders. Similarly, to be depressed a great deal of the time may be a sign of an emotional problem that needs treatment.

We have spoken of the insights of Christian thinkers who trace the roots of mental disorders to the general human condition we call sin. The Danish philosopher, Soren Kierkegaard, observed that despair means a recognition of a lack of possibility, a shutting of the self within the self. Despair, which is a deep form of depression, thus shows a lack of a good relationship with God and other people.

It's important to note that those of us who fall into depression, or who may develop emotional illnesses, are not more sinful than others, but may only be more aware of the state of sin than others. Kierkegaard, who thought long about the religious condition, rather harshly said that suffering is a way of coming to the real meaning of the Christian faith. He also said that most people do not feel sick enough to accept faith. Most of us want to depend on ourselves, even when we really can't handle our problems. Such self-centeredness really causes depressed feelings.

With this warning in mind, that those of us who fall sick are not more sinful than others, we may examine some of the symptoms of depression. Depression, like unhappiness, is a loaded word. It needs to be unpacked and defined. Generally speaking, we are all aware when we feel "blue," but we may not know why.

Depression, like most emotional disorders, is only an exaggerated expression of quite common human emotional states. It is not being just unhappy, but rather deeply unhappy without the ability to throw off that uncomfortable feeling. Depression includes sadness, loneliness, pessimism, and uncertainty. The emotional energy needed to go out of the self and begin new activities, to make friends, or even to apologize to others, is lacking. There is a vague feeling that everything is wrong, and no matter what one might do, if one felt like doing anything, it would go wrong, too.

Some of us who are depressed feel an intense pain. Not a physical pain, but pain over not being able to respond to any stimulus. We look upon persons and things and feel unable to derive pleasure from any of them. This can lead to feelings of self-pity that provoke sudden outbursts of tears. But while some men and women will cry, others will not. Indeed, some of us are not even aware that we are depressed. We may feel irritable, or even become angry easily, but we credit these states to the difficulties of our job, or to crises in the family. Our depression is then hidden from us and becomes a source of real difficulties with others, in that we may put blame on other people for doing things that upset us so.

Of course, fatigue can promote depression. Boredom with routine, a sense of being trapped in a meaningless life style, frustration at being unable to change a situation that the mind knows should be changed—all these situations can contribute to depression. But such real conditions are not always the case.

In general, we may follow the analysis of Dr. Nathan S. Kline, who suggests that the classic syndrome or group of symptoms that point to the existence of depression in a person include:

—Reduced enjoyment in pleasure. This symptom is always found in a depression.

—Poor concentration. We may forget what we have read or heard as soon as we have done so.

—Fatigue. A feeling of constant tiredness.

—Insomnia. We may find it difficult to sleep or wake up after only an hour or two of sleep.

114

—Remorse.

—Guilt. Because we cannot function as we would ordinarily, we might feel guilty about that.

—Indecision. An inability to make up our mind.

—Financial concern.

—Reduced social activities. We may lose all interest in sex. We take no pleasure in parties and friends.

—Decreased love and affection.

—General loss of interest.

—Anxiety. We may feel so anxious that others may think that anxiety is our problem rather than depression.

—Irritability. Trivial things may upset us.

—Suicidal thoughts. Such thoughts of self-destruction can be very frightening.

—Unusual thoughts and urges. Sometimes one fears a loved one will die.

—Physical changes. Changes in bowel habits and loss of appetite are common. Sometimes there is a loss of weight. But other people may overeat. Diarrhea, constipation, nausea, chest pains, stomach cramps, rapid breathing, sweating, coldness of the hands and feet, or numbness of the hands and feet may be experienced. Quite commonly, headaches or a feeling of pressure in the head may be experienced.

—Concern about dying. Because of the changes in one's overall condition, and the physical problems that may accompany it, the person may feel that he is dying of a terrible disease.[3]

There are other signs of depression, as well, but these may only be read by one who is familiar with the person's usual life style. The person may speak with difficulty. He may respond to conversation with difficulty. Also, he may be messy in dress and personal cleanliness. His figure may droop and he may be clumsy in walking. However, all of these things might be the natural style of someone, so they don't necessarily mean depression as such. Real changes in one's ordinary life style must be looked for.

To say that our lives are full of sorrow and pain is ridiculous, unless we are imprisoned or suffering from a terrible disease. Yet it is true, as Henry David Thoreau remarked in *Walden*, that many people "lead lives of quiet desperation."

It is not so much that we hurt inside all the time; our problem is that we hurt all too often. Nothing can deliver us from the common problems and aches of life, but something, surely, can be done about the surplus of suffering in millions of lives.

"Quiet desperation" is as good a description of despair, of depression, as we are likely to get. We need to look seriously at what psychiatrists and psychologists can tell us about the depression syndrome. As Dr. Kline observes, there are three different kinds of depression that may be troubling us, or a member of our family.

First, there is biological depression. This is the most common type, caused by a chemical imbalance in the brain. Treatment for it is available in the form of drugs that change the metabolism of the brain. For the thousands who suffer from this disease, nothing more serious than medical care is needed. The answer to the problem, then is counseling the affected person to see a doctor immediately.

The second form of depression is neurotic, caused by internal stress. Frustration, failure, rejection (or at least what the mind considers rejection) lie at the base of this disease. Counseling or psychotherapy, coupled with drug treatment, can deal with the problem. Only a well-trained physician can tell just what is the underlying cause of one's depression, however.

The third form of depression is existential, caused by external stress. Bickering in the home, falling out with

116

friends, breaking one's word to another, all can cause this form of depression. Once again, only the physician can judge what is causing a particular depressed episode.

The good news about all these forms of depression is that they all respond to treatment by new medical preparations. One can be helped up and out of a depressed state.

Living Then, Now

Of far more interest to the lay Christian who would struggle against unhappiness in himself and in others, is the type of hurt that results from living in the past. This form of bondage to ancient mistakes is more common than we may realize.

A recent mystery story involved several murders among a group of Eastern European exiles living in New York City. The investigator tried to find out if communist agents had committed these crimes, or if exiled freedom fighters had, perhaps, killed some traitors in their own group. The solution turned out to be very different.

One of the murder victims was a former Hungarian freedom fighter, who wore his Hungarian Army uniform at rallies. The murderer turned out to be an eighty-year-old man who had fought the Austro-Hungarian army more than sixty years before. He killed in the name of "Croatia," a country that had not existed for over sixty years! This was a life of unhappiness truly controlled by the past. To show that truth is stranger than fiction, the fall, 1976 skyjacking of an American airplane was done by a group dedicated to the freedom of Croatia! Our happiness or unhappiness really depends more on the past than we would like to think.

The technical name for this situation is psychological determinism. To some degree, we are trying to control the past by living in unusual, nonresponsible ways now. Many more of us react to people and events in the present because of feelings carried over from the past than may realize it.

There is the case of the woman who regularly ignored her husband, showing him no affection. The man fell into the same pattern and ignored her. Everything went along smoothly, but not happily, until the man sought counseling help. When the husband tried to communicate and show affection to his wife, she rejected him. She was upset, preferring to live in silence. When the wife was brought into analysis, it developed that she had loved her father so much that she wished (in her child-mind) that her mother would die so she could have her father all to herself. (This is fairly common among children.) Unfortunately, her mother did die, and in a state of guilt and grief, she "turned off" her affection for her father. She punished herself by being cold to him, and later, substituted her husband (in her mind) for her father.

Such people will marry people who remind them of the person they tried to control or manipulate in the past. The husband could have gone on through life, miserable, living out the childhood script this wife had written for herself and her father, if he hadn't begun to hurt so badly that he sought medical help.

Now is now and then is then. We need to stop punishing ourselves for things we wished for—or even did—in childhood and adolescence. If we are ever to find happiness in the present, we need freedom from the past.

There is only one way this freedom can be secured— through forgiveness. We must ask God for his forgiveness through Christ and sincerely have faith that God has granted it. We must, then, have the courage to forgive others, whether they are now living or dead, who may have sinned against us in the past. Then we must have the openness of spirit to forgive ourselves since Christ has truly forgiven us.

Only forgiveness in Christ can free us from the dead past.

Not Who We Are But Who We Would Be Brings Us Pain

Dietrich Bonhoeffer's attempt to understand the Christian gospel and its implications for his life brought him not worldly success, but death in a Nazi concentration camp. Fame came to Bonhoeffer, but only after he was hanged by the Gestapo and his ashes scattered to the winds. Though young, Dietrich left a valuable body of Christian writings for those who would follow him in faith. Some of his last letters from prison speak of a "world come of age" and of the need for a "religionless Christianity." Many of those who have read these letters have been offended while others have rejoiced and embraced secularism. Both groups of readers have misunderstood Dietrich Bonhoeffer's point.

What Bonhoeffer actually meant in his writings is very much to the point of our desire to find a way from places and deeds that hurt us to a life of Christian joy. For Bonhoeffer did find joy, joy in Christ, not by the avoidance of the cross but by embracing it.

Just before his execution, Bonhoeffer led a simple worship service for other prisoners. All remarked on the comfort his words gave them. Dietrich seemed at peace. As the service broke up, Bonhoeffer told one man, a British officer, "This is the end for me, the beginning of life."

These are easy words to say—or to write—but hard to bear. Bonhoeffer's words are understandable only to those who have passed through their own dark night of the soul, known their own suffering, and turned it all over to God. He echoes the stout confession of the theologian, Karl Barth, whom he knew. Barth declared:

"The end of life is not death but resurrection."

Once more these are good words to say, but difficult to truly mean. We cannot make of Christianity a religion of cheap grace. Such declarations can be heartfelt only by those who have known Jesus' cross as a part of their own lives.

Someone has said that pain is an angel, for through pain human beings have been moved to the most profound self-insight and appreciation of the simple things of life. A man who has lost a finger may feel sorry for himself until he meets a man with no hand. I have had this sort of experience. Twice I made the journey from the battlefield to the aid station, to the evacuation helicopter, to the divisional hospital, to the hospital ship, and then by plane to base hospitals in another country. At each stop along the evacuation chain one meets more and more people who have suffered worse injuries than he has. Even a big hurt takes on perspective when one meets the blind or the multiple amputee.

Yet there is more to finding joy in pain than becoming aware of the sufferings of others. Undoubtedly, there are always others who are in worse condition than we are, or at least the odds are on that side. But if this were all there were to mature acceptance of pain and loss, then hell would be heaven, for one could see unimaginable sufferings in hell, yet be no happier for it.

Seeing the reality of how life treats others can give us perspective upon our own hurts, that is true. And in some of us it can move us to profound sympathy with others who suffer. Even the hardest of men try to be gentle with the seriously injured. Fellow-feeling, the solidarity of the human race, brotherly love, are seen quite often in the brutality of war or the tragedy of a train wreck.

Yet there is more. Not only perspective on our own hurt but the courage and imagination to grasp our hurt and use it to grow is needed also. Give one person a piece of wood and he will look at it and lay it aside. Give a similar piece of wood to another person and he will carve a statue from it. We can take the raw materials of our own fears, depressions, anxieties, loneliness, and suffering—and mold from these experiences something beautiful, wise, and good. It can be done, although it cannot be done alone.

As children we are caught by the lovely stories of Christmas. The songs of Bethlehem and the declarations of the angels thrill us. We love the box of straw and the sweet baby Jesus within it. The shepherds, the ox, and the ass move us. But we find the story of Christ's passion difficult to grasp. We cannot fathom why men beat Jesus with whips, fashioned a cross, made him carry it stumbling through the streets and, finally, nailed that good man to a cross, hands and feet. Why? How could people hate Jesus when he only did good? Why would anyone do so?

I don't think we can fully understand the Passion until we are mature enough to know suffering ourselves. We cannot really see that the manger and the cross are inseparably connected, that the wood of the baby's box is the same wood that forms his cross.

Why? Because Jesus' life is one of love and love is a state of suffering, although it is suffering transformed into joy. The Book of Hebrews puts it plainly, ". . . for the joy that was set before him (Jesus) endured the cross, despising the shame . . ." (Heb. 12:2).

Suffering is redemptive. It heals. It heals not everyone who suffers, but it heals those who see it as the raw material out of which to fashion a life of blessings to others and of glory to God.

We need to embrace, not reject the many pains that come to us daily. We need to value, not deny and try to forget the hurts that fall upon us like Shakespeare's famous "slings and arrows" of fortune. We need to test each anguish and ask it, "What can you teach me?" We must examine every rejection, asking: "What are you trying to tell me?" As the physician notes each symptom and seeks to diagnose the hidden condition of his patient, we, too, must take every hurt seriously so as to determine the state of our spirits.

Paul knew this. So did James. "Count it all joy . . . when you meet various trials," James declares (1:2) Paul wanted to fill up Christ's sufferings with his own. He knew that the thorn in his flesh was given to teach him something about the meaning of a life lived under the grace of a good God (2 Cor. 12:7).

Dietrich Bonhoeffer also knew that suffering heals, and hurts examined make one mature. Bonhoeffer's theology is called a "theology of reality," because he taught that we ought never to look at the world without seeing God in the midst of it, or never to think of God without thinking of God's presence in the midst of the world. Not what ought to be, nor what might be, but what is, tells us of God and his plans for us. Here, in the center of this world, in the midst of our joys and sufferings, God calls us to bear witness to the saving cross. Here, in the place where we are set, even if that is a concentration camp, we are to be Christ's disciples, to follow after him, bearing our own cross. Happiness is to be found not in escaping from reality, but in embracing it. The sweet taste of life does not come from licking its surface, as if it were an ice cream cone or an all-day sucker, but by biting into its hard substance, which nourishes us with its bittersweet flesh.

Right here. Right now. God is here. Joy is here. Peace is here, if I will stick with life, trust God in Christ, and wait for those blessings to come to fruition.

Edgar Lee Masters has one of the ghosts of the pioneers in his *Spoon River Anthology* declare:

"Degenerate sons and daughters! It takes life to live life."

No one ever promised us a rose garden. No one was ever guaranteed a happy-go-lucky ride through life. As Siddahartha, who became the Buddha, was to learn, despite the attempts of his father to shield him from all the "ugly" aspects of life, human life contains sickness, suffering, old age, and death. That is life, by definition.

Yet many of us today act as if we do not know that we are desperately unhappy—not because of what we are but because of who we would be. We are sad and troubled, not because of what we have, but because of what we would have. We reject the reality we are given by God in favor of an unreality we mistakenly prefer. The husband or wife we have is not "right" for us, so we would have another. The job we have does not suit us, but another job would. Our children disappoint us, they are not like someone else's children. The possessions we have are not "good" enough for us, we would have grander things.

No matter how hard a husband or wife tries to be a good spouse, one will never be happy with him or her, for one is wedded to unreality. No matter how important our job, it can never satisfy us for we are contracted to an unreal vision of our vocation. No matter how fine our possessions, they cannot satisfy, for we carry a vision of a pseudo-world around inside our heads. We are unhappy and no one is allowed to take that state away from us. Married to the wind, we are tied to illusion, lustful for the unreal, the utopian, the "nowhere," and the "never was."

In Bonhoeffer's insightful theological terms, we have rejected God's reality—and our fellowman. Fleeing from the concrete world of work and play, fellowship and pain, suffering and joy, we have sought for an unreal world that exists only in the illusions of a selfish mind. We have displaced this world, the place of God's incarnation in Christ. The spot where Christ has built his church as a testimony to his abiding presence among us is not good enough for us.

We can never be happy until we give up unreality and embrace the real world of everyday, with its fuel crises, cold weather, runny noses, political campaigns, and dirty children. Until we take up the cross of the hurts this real world visits upon us, and follow the Christ who is the hidden heart and perfect center of this imperfect world, we can never know joy. For it is in turning our full attention to the world that spreads out on every side around us that we will find joy:

123

joy that is more than happiness, for joy is the acceptance of suffering, a satisfaction that lasts beyond the time of laughter and beyond the time for tears.

Not Religion But Faith Gives Peace and Joy

Religion is the clearest expression of human sin, declares Karl Barth, the Swiss Reformed theologian, and Dietrich Bonhoeffer, the German Lutheran martyr. Such a declaration amazes and confounds us, for we have long been taught that religion is good and the sources of answers to the problems that beset us. Yet Barth and Bonhoeffer are good Christians and good churchmen. They must have something important in mind.

They do. What these theologians are saying is that religion is a human work, a man-made effort. Religion is humanity's attempt to find God—and to please God by man's good works. As such a practice, religion grows out of humanity's fears and longings, out of man's cares and needs. It is not love but fear that propels the religious impulse. Religion is built upon human anxiety and consequently can never relieve anxiety.

No one recognized this fact about religion more clearly than Martin Luther, the great Protestant Reformer. Reared in a pious medieval Catholic home, Luther was religious to the extreme. He fasted, beat his body, and prayed. Nothing seemed to help his sensitive conscience. Luther agonized over his question, "How can I find a merciful God?" Finally, Luther was blessed by an understanding of Paul's teaching about faith in the New Testament. Religion, the way of works and efforts, is not the path. Rather, faith—not a series of beliefs but an attitude of trust—in God's grace shown to mankind in Christ is the way to salvation. Faith is not the same as religion, but is its opposite. Faith trusts God; it is not anxious to please him, or to prove his existence. Faith takes for granted the goodness of God and his benevolent disposition toward us, for such is Jesus' message and the example of his life, death, and resurrection. Faith does not assume but feels assured that the world around it is already inhabited by Christ's presence. Reality is centered by Christ, just as time is divided and measured by Christ's incarnation. As this is the twentieth century after Christ's coming, even so the world around us is centered on Christ and receives its structure and meaning from him. Many human beings in this world may not understand this, but the person of faith does. God does not change his behavior because of human unfaith, after all.

Beyond Religious Answers

To surrender to God in Christ, to simply rest upon his cross and promise, is the way to move through pain, hurt, and suffering to the experience of happiness and the condition of joy. To stop trying, to relax anxieties, to stop trying "to prove something" to either oneself, other people, or God is "the way to freedom." To accept the reality of God within the broken, pain-filled, sinful reality around one is the way to move beyond hurt to responsible joy.

Bonhoeffer believed that such faith meant responsible discipleship. To see God in his world is to see God as suffering, as taking part in the weakness and pain of his children. To see Christ as the center of the world is to see Christ carrying his cross, and to feel the need to respond by "taking up the cross" and following our Lord.

To persons with faith, to us when we surrender to the loving Christ, the world is seen through fresh eyes. We see that crime, selfishness, and sinfulness not only hurt the neighbor man but strike God in the eye and drive another spike through Christ's mangled hands. To see God as suffering in us and through us and with us is to affirm suffering, pain, loneliness, and hurt. To affirm our hurt is to transform it from a burden to a privilege, the opportunity of

125

suffering with God. To transform our suffering is to redeem it—to see it as a sacramental means of communion with God.

Apart from the identification of our hurts with the sufferings of Christ, there is no true remedy for them. We may forget our pains of spirit for a while in troubled sleep, repress them with psychological denial, drown them with alcoholic intoxication, or mask them with drug abuse, but we cannot heal our own hurts in these ways or any others.

The Body of Christ

When we respond in faith to the Christ who stands at the center of the world around us, we lose the bitter edge of our loneliness because we are propelled by his Spirit toward his body—the church. God fills the world, to be sure; he is found in every part of it, but he is found—by those who do not have faith—as wrath against sin. Only in the church is God found as grace and forgiveness.

Christ struggles with sin and redeems suffering in the world and provides the strength to persevere in our weakness through the sacramental community, the church.

The Holy Spirit

To see God in the world and Christ as the world's center is to see Christ's body, the church, not as a place apart, but as the very structure of the world. The church was established by God in his call to Abraham in the Old Testament, by his securing of a peculiar people as witnesses to his saving acts in history. This chosen people, Israel, chosen for service, not out of favoritism, were not a people apart from the world, but entered fully into the world's activities and conflicts. The God of Abraham, Isaac, and Jacob is the God of history, the God of reality, the only true God. The Lord does not call us out of the world but into the world as his witnesses and co-workers. In the New Testament, God's covenant with his chosen people is renewed. We have a new covenant, made in Jesus Christ, God's true High Priest and perfect witness. The church Jesus founds on the faith of Peter and the other apostles is the new Israel. Once more, in the Book of Acts we see the church as very much involved in the affairs of the world.

Peter, Stephen, and other apostolic men and women preached in the streets, calling all, far and near, to faith in Jesus Christ, who was the consummation of God's promises contained in the Hebrew Scriptures. These involved apostles were dragged before the law courts and the legislative bodies of the day because they would not let the public world alone. They did not see Christianity as something an individual does with his own time. They did not see faith in Christ as a rapture out of the world or a call to abandon the affairs of the world. Rather the apostles bore witness to Christ by bearing his cross and sharing in his suffering in the daily life of the marketplace, the courtroom, the ship on a voyage, and even in prison itself. Like their Lord, Jesus Christ, many of these apostolic faithful also met death at the hands of mobs. Stephen, deacon and martyr, stands as a symbol for all those who identified fully with the sufferings of Christ. "Lord," Stephen prays, "do not hold this sin against them" (Acts 7:60). Stephen is the picture of a person who has moved through rejection, pain, hatred, and suffering to see his suffering as part of Christ's suffering that lies at the heart of all life, as its inner meaning. Stephen, whose death moved many to faith, shows us the redemptiveness of Christian suffering.

Stephen's death also shows us the meaning of the church, the communion of saints, the mother of martyrs. To be a member of the church is to be baptized into Christ's death and resurrected to a new, eternal life in him. To be part of the church is to be incorporated into Christ's very body, as a limb or organ is part of a man. To be a Christian is to have

127

Christ in us, in a spiritual indwelling, and to know that we are in Christ, part of his ever-living body, the church. This is a visible church—Christ is the world's very structure and the church, flung far and wide and found at every level and dimension of social life, is the concrete expression of Christ's structure. Of course, not every structure of the church is a direct structure of Christ. Indeed, some such church structures may be structures of destruction. Yet the Christian has no right to be cynical. Anything that is good in intention and does good for mankind, must be seen as stemming from Christ. Whatever good there is in the world comes from Christ. He is the foundation and structure of all good. Christ functions in this way as the antithesis of evil, and communicates his healing, helping power through his Holy Spirit.

The church is the workshop of Christ's Holy Spirit. The Spirit is located wherever the gospel of Christ is rightly preached and the sacraments of Christ (through which symbols Christ is revealed to us) are rightly administered. The Spirit is always connected to the work of Christ, for as Jesus Christ points out in John's Gospel, the Spirit takes the elements of Christ's work and makes them understandable to men and women. Christ's Holy Spirit is the revelation of the inward will of God toward man. The Spirit is the power and the form of freely given love. The Spirit is the Spirit of the church because it is the Spirit of forgiveness.

Paul tells us, in his great theological work, the Epistle to the Romans, that the Holy Spirit bears witness to our spirit that we are children of God. The divine Spirit groans as we groan and the very fabric of the material universe groans under the sufferings produced by sin, selfishness, and narrowness. Just as we may offer up our pain, our hurt, our loneliness, our anxiety, and our suffering to Christ, and see ourselves as united with him in a suffering like his, even so the Holy Spirit identifies with our suffering. Our pain, therefore, not only now has meaning and is transcended and redeemed, but also is made possible by the agreement with our spirits of the Divine Spirit. We are given the strength to bear what faith shows us must be borne. By the Spirit's power we are able to endure and to grow in faith and love.

The Book of Hebrews speaks of "the rest" that the Christian finds in God (Heb. 4:9, 10). This rest is the repose, the peace of spirit that a person finds in the assurance of faith. To stop seeking release and relief elsewhere, to cease striving for happiness on one's own, to be "in" Christ's body, the church, is the one sure way of being in a state of happiness beyond hurt.

The church is a frequently praised and a more frequently criticized institution. It probably sounds strange to suggest active church involvement as the solution to our problems of hurt and pain. Nevertheless, this is precisely the advice now being given.

To live in a state of happiness beyond hurt, we must live by daily forgiveness, by daily forgetting, by daily caring, while seeing the world with the fresh eyes that come with faith in Christ. Paradoxically, uniquely, strangely, this state comes only when we understand:

That to stop seeking
is the way to find;
That to forget oneself
is to possess oneself truly;
To start working for others
is to find rest for oneself
And to sleep, to rest, is to dream and to dare.

To relax at the oars of life's boat, but to keep on rowing steadily, assured that God's waves will push us to land, is the way of rest (peace, faith) in the church. To be busy and not rushed, tired but not weary, responsible but not harried, is the way of happiness beyond hurt.

This is possible only in the *koinonia*, the fellowship of Christ's church. *Koinonia* is a Greek word that means communion in the common fellowship of those called to faith in Christ. The word "church" comes from the Greek term, *ecclesia*, which means "those called out," those whom God has called to faith in Christ. This called communion is, indeed, the mystical body of Christ.

The Church is Christ's body in that it is the concrete expression of his living spirit stretched out in time and space. The church is the sign and channel of Christ's love spread out all over the face of the globe. If we truly believe this and are a living part of it ourselves, then no hurt can shake our faith and no anxiety can last for long in a life that is busy about God's business.

Overcoming Hurt

Overcoming Hurt

As we have seen, hurt is a universal experience. I hurt, you hurt, we all hurt, and more, most of us recognize this situation. Only the youngest of children or the shallowest thinkers among adults believe that other people do not have these common human miseries and anxieties. Edwin Arlington Robinson's poem, "Richard Cory," is an ironic comment on shallow minds who believe that someone is happy because he is good-looking and wealthy. Beneath the smiles or frowns people wear are similar sufferings; pains caused by the same dynamics in other lives that work in ours.

> Whenever Richard Cory went downtown,
>   We people on the pavement looked at him:
> He was a gentleman from sole to crown,
>   Clean favored, and imperially slim.
>
> And he was always quietly arrayed,
>   And he was always human when he talked;
> But still he fluttered pulses when he said,
>   "Good-morning," and he glittered when he walked.
>
> And he was rich—yes, richer than a king—
>   And admirably schooled in every grace:

In fine, we thought that he was everything
  To make us wish that we were in his place.

So on we worked, and waited for the light,
  And went without the meat, and cursed the bread;
And Richard Cory, one calm summer night,
  Went home and put a bullet through his head. [1]

The legend of the awakening of the Buddha points to this truth. The young prince who was to become Buddha was riding in his coach one day and saw several unfortunate people along India's roadsides. The prince saw a beggar, a sick man, an aged wanderer, and a dead person. He concluded that life was full of poverty, sickness, old age, and death. Buddha was not wrong. Life is hard. Life is tough and leaves scars on all of us. We all hurt.

A natural question arises, "How can we overcome hurt?" And a natural answer is that we cannot do it alone. So many times we hurt ourselves and others by our own actions designed to help, but we cannot overcome hurt that way. Hurt is something for the Healer, for God as we know him in Christ. But God works through means in our world. God will help us overcome hurt, if we ask him to do so, by working through our friends, our loved ones, and through ourselves. We need others as they need us, but we need the God who works through them even more.

As we must all recognize, we cannot overcome hurt by ourselves, and yet the key to identifying what hurts us, who hurts us, and how we are hurting ourselves, and how we are hurting others, does lie within ourselves. It is more than simply a pious phrase to say that only God can overcome hurt. This is the truth, because only God who gave us life can restore life when it has gone awry. But God works through means in this world; he works from the means of other people, most particularly, our loved ones and our friends, our ministers and counselors, our teachers, those whom we respect, perhaps through the professions, such as

134

medicine, the law, and psychiatry. But God is not limited to the means of other people for he can also work through us. This is what is meant when we say that healing our hurt must, in some sense, originate with us. Not in our own reason and strength, as Luther tells us, are we saved, but in the God whom we find within when we look and pray and have faith that he is there. We need others, but we need more to come to grips with ourselves. More than we need to come to grips with ourselves, we need God's power. We need to tap the healing power of Christ.

From time to time in the history of Christianity, healing by faith has become well-known and popular. At other times, perhaps most times in the history of the church, healing by faith is something to which all people give lip service, but in which they put little credence. Times in which faith healing, if we want to call it that, has been very prominent in the church seem to have been the very earliest days of the church as recorded in Acts, and in the Middle Ages, in association with the great shrines to which people made pilgrimages, (such as Lourdes and other places in Europe). Surprisingly enough, in the last decade or so, there is a resurgence of healing in the United States and Canada. This kind of faith healing is often associated with evangelists and others who have special services of prayer and the anointing of people with oil, or laying on of hands, or the healing of various kinds of physical diseases or physical injuries, perhaps even psychological trauma. Now I'm not about to depreciate that kind of healing by faith or to suggest that it is the only kind of healing there is. In the main, God works through the means he has chosen and ordained in the world; for our purposes that would be through the means of psychiatry or psychology, medicine in all its many branches, and the counseling arts. Yet we must never forget that God is God, the Sovereign. He could work in ways he himself would elect. I am not, in this book, suggesting that some unusual form of healing by faith is necessary to overcome the hurts of life. Just as we have been most concerned to discuss the kinds of hurts that are common to all human beings, the kinds of everyday hurts in distinction from the very outstanding kinds of crises and injuries that can come to us, I'm concerned to stress the everyday, ordinary miracle of healing by faith.

Martin Luther once preached a sermon on miracles that talked about the man who had been born blind. He spoke about the wonderful power that Jesus showed when he healed this man and gave him his eyesight again. But then Luther suggested that perhaps people who hear this story are lusting after miracles in their own hearts; lusting after unusual occurrences of God's power and forgetting the everyday miracle of life itself. Luther certainly believed in God's power and the reality of miracles, but he suggested that when we become fixed upon unusual kinds of healing we forget the one who is healed. For Luther it was a miracle that we can see at all, and hear, touch, feel, taste, and smell. Give thanks for this great miracle of healing, he says, that the man born blind can now see through Jesus' power. But give thanks that you can see, and that you can see yesterday, and you will be able to see tomorrow as well. This is the true miracle—the miracle of every day, the miracle we constantly overlook and forget in unfaith.

It is to this common, ordinary, everyday, yet nevertheless, miraculous power of God, that I am pointing. We will not forget that there are those who will be healed in an unusual way, but we must remember that which they are restored to, their good health, their happiness. We take those ordinary things for granted and yet nevertheless they are miraculous gifts from Almighty God.

In the Christian vocabulary, no word is used more than the word saved or salvation. Yet many times we are not clear about what we mean by being saved, or having experienced salvation. As someone has pointed out, we ought to ask what we have been saved from, and saved for, when we use this word. In the orthodox Christian conception, in that system of theology which runs through all of the reformers and teachers of the church, we read that we are saved by grace through faith, from the power of sin, death, the law, and the devil.

We are saved from some mighty important and terribly strong powers. It is not just from some natural, everyday occurrences, as someone might be picked out of the water and thus saved by a sailor in a boat. Rather, we are saved from the forces and demonic powers that can warp our lives and very definitely hurt us and those around us. We are saved from sin. And sin is not just simply a list of things we do or don't do, things forbidden or commanded, but sin is a power. It is a power and spirit of rebellion against God. We need to be saved from this power. And we are saved, too, from death.

This may seem strange, since all of us will see death in our own time and no one is exempt from dying. But the death that the New Testament speaks of is more than physical death. Physical death will have its overcoming, also, when the resurrection of the dead is accomplished at the end of time. Yet we are saved from death in the here and now before we also taste physical death. Death is the state of being separated from God. This separation is the sting of death. It is associated with the law and the breaking of the law. This is the death that Jesus Christ's own death has overcome and made into eternal life itself.

It may seem strange to say that we are delivered from the power of the law, that we are saved from the law. We can understand, against the backdrop of the traditional Christian language, how being saved from the power of the devil is a reality. But to say that we are saved from the law seems somehow strange. Nevertheless, this is the language of Paul in Romans and elsewhere. We are saved from the law as a power; we are saved from the law as a means of trying to save ourselves. For, as Paul points out, if there were any law,

which by the keeping of it, could give us life, then Jesus
Christ died in vain. But in fact there is no such law.

There is no sense and no way in which we could perfectly
fulfill even the Ten Commandments, much less the whole
will of God rooted in his law which is written upon our very
hearts, according to Romans 1. Delivered from the law, we
are no longer under the bondage of obligation and duty—
we are delivered from the law which binds us to God, but in
the way of a debtor to one to whom he owes a debt. We are
delivered from the law, for our transgressions are forgiven
and our sins are called as white as wool, when we believe in
Christ. And we are delivered from the devil, for as the sting
of death is the sting that is in the law, and the breaking of it,
even so the devil is the power that uses our inability to keep
the law against us. The devil is the symbol of all those forces
of demonic power that stand over against God and his will.
The devil, as the accuser of man, who keeps us constantly
in the state of a bad conscience, is the tempter, who leads us
into testing. We are delivered from his power by the blood
of Christ. Thus we are saved from the law and from death,
and from sin and from the devil.

We are saved by the blood of Christ. In the original
language, salvation means healing. The Latin, *salvus*, from
which we get the English word, salve, means to heal. We
need to recognize that all salvation is healing. It is a restoration of that which once was good and fine, and healthy and
whole, but which has been damaged by sin. Salvation is
healing from the disease of rebellion against God. To experience this salvation, we must have faith in it. We must
have faith to believe that we have broken, by our own sin, as
well as original sin, the cord that binds us to God. And we
must believe that God can restore this relationship to himself again, that he can reconcile us to himself through Jesus
Christ. We must have faith that the blood of Jesus Christ
cleanses us from all sin. He who has seen Christ, has seen
the Father. This must be our belief, our confidence.

When we are hurt, when we truly feel the pain and the hurting, it would be more than a simple pious exercise to spend some time reading the Passion Story of Jesus in the Gospels. It would be well to review the great Suffering Servant songs of the prophet Isaiah (Isa. 52 and 53), where we read the magnificent words, "Surely he has borne our griefs and carried our sorrows; yet we esteemed him stricken, smitten by God and afflicted. But he was wounded for our transgressions, and he was bruised for our iniquities" (Isa. 53:4, 5). These words come true in the Passion Story. Jesus has borne our griefs. Jesus is the Healer, and the Healer deals with hurt. Perhaps we have not stressed this enough.

There has been a strain of thought in Christianity called triumphalism. We have spoken much of the victory of Christ and have used the power derived from Christ in a very triumphant way. Thinking ourselves in some sense morally superior to others, we have sought to be their teachers. Now there is a great truth in the fact that Christ is victor and that he has triumphed over all the powers of hell. But we need to look again at the Healer. The Healer is one who deals with hurt. "I have come to seek and to save the lost," Jesus said. I have not come for the righteous, but I've come to seek and save that which is lost. "He went about doing good" is what we say about Jesus Christ. He went about doing good, true, but primarily Jesus came to deal with sin and its consequences. This means that in his earthly life he was concerned not so much to be triumphant as King, he was concerned to be the Healer and Helper of men.

Of course, Jesus' time and attention were not primarily given to the healing of bodies, or even of disturbed souls in his day. He had come to deal with the basis of all those hurts, with man's bondage to sin. Yet so much is he the Healer, so much is he concerned with hurt, that Jesus could not forbear touching this one here and this one there, and healing them, even bringing people back from the dead.

Jesus was concerned with hurt. His followers were not perfect people or paragons of morality. They were not athletic, healthy people—they were people with hurts. They were drawn to him because they had hurts. Because they had hurts, he healed them. "Did not our hearts leap for joy when he broke the bread for us?" the disciples said after Jesus' resurrection. Jesus and Christianity have to do with hurts, not glorying in them, not morbid preoccupation with them, but dealing with hurts to heal them.

This is the faith that leads to joy. This kind of faith does not see life as something all unraveled, and all its problems solved, but it sees that in the very heart of God there is concern for human hurts and a concern for human welfare. It is a concern for that which is good—a concern for overcoming hurt among Christians, in God. God wants people who hurt themselves to change and go about doing good.

A father saw his little boy run out into the busy street, called him back, and gave him a sound spanking. When the child cried and looked hurt, the father explained, "It's for your own good."

Children often have to cope with that phrase. How many times were you faced with a tablespoonful of castor oil, or some foul-tasting medicine—only to be told, "It will do you good"?

The experience doesn't end with childhood. Read the letters to the editors in the newspapers. Someone is always denouncing a movie, a play, or a book—for the "good" of the community. Politicians and commentators, and even neighbors, invariably know what is "good" for us. And we cannot help but think that Hitler justified his murder of freedom in Germany by saying it was for the people's own "good."

Not surprisingly, we tend to resent some kinds of "good" that are done for us. We are often suspicious of those who want to do us "good." So we may want to take a second look when the Scriptures tell us that Jesus "went about doing good."

To clear our minds, and get a true perspective on what is truly good, we need to consider the actual ministry of Jesus. When we read the Gospels, we find that Christ acted in kindness and out of compassion.

Who could imagine accomplishing anything in such a meek, considerate way? We have so often seen what men call justice done by gunfire, by compulsion and force, that a gentle justice astounds us. Perhaps it should not, since the recent years of bloodshed in that very area where Jesus lived his life have seemed to produce neither peace nor justice.

Force was not Jesus' style. Nor was command. In fact, John tells us that when a large group of people mistakenly sought to pay him honor by making him king, Jesus simply went away (John 6:15). The good that Jesus does is not done by force or fiat. We cannot imagine Jesus doing something for someone's "own good" against that person's will.

In the Book of Acts, Paul says that "God anointed Jesus of Nazareth with the Holy Spirit and with power; how he went about doing good and healing all that were oppressed by the devil, for God was with him" (Acts 10:38).

That is quite a Messiah! If, by the power of God, Jesus did good by healing, by making people whole, through love and not force, his gospel is good news. And it is. Jesus comes to do people good by doing for them, according to their own needs, not by shaping them according to some outside standard called "good."

How often the Bible reminds us of the humility and humanity, the kindness of Jesus and his identification of himself with the common people. At the very beginning of his ministry, Jesus went to John, who was preaching by the Jordan River, and was baptized along with the mass of common sinners. Jesus never broke a reed of personality that was already strained to the breaking point by sin. He never put out the light of a sincere repentance that was just

141

bursting into flame in a sinner's breast. In the case of the woman taken in the very act of adultery, Jesus did not condemn the poor creature "for her own good," but recognized the common weakness of humanity, calling for him "who is without sin" to cast the first stone.

Jesus, our Savior, was not and is not too good to be the Friend and Helper of weak and needy sinners like you and me. His gentle healing is demonstrated by his acceptance of us as we are. Jesus does not condone sin. He condemns it. But he affirms the humanity and the possibility of change for the sinner.

Two thousand years have passed since Jesus stood in the shallow Jordan River and let John baptize him. We still celebrate that incredible act today. But in the intervening years some of us have forgotten the kind of humanity, the divine humanity of the One who identified with the poor, the hurt, and the sinful, and who sought to do genuine good to all he met. Some of us have forgotten to help the bruised reeds we meet. We despise the dimly burning wicks we see spluttering around us. And we are remiss in doing justice, rendering to everyone of his due and his respect. We are thoughtless and selfish—far from being like the Jesus revealed in the Scriptures.

If we were like him, we would go about doing good—not as we see it, but as people need it.

Johnny Appleseed is a historical figure familiar to millions of schoolchildren. For many people who live in the Midwest, he is more than that. Johnny Appleseed's legacy of love, the hundreds of fruit trees he planted in his wandering across the face of the land, still may be seen. Johnny was a simple man; he desired no power over others, not even the power to change people's minds. He wanted to do genuine good for people, so he planted apple seeds. And the trees that grew became a blessing to all those whose paths he crossed.

Once we begin to reflect upon the truly loving among

people, upon those marked in their deepest character by Jesus' unselfish spirit, our thoughts begin to soar. We think of the gentle St. Francis of Assisi, who bathed and cared for the victims of the plague without regard for his own safety; we remember his quiet goodness that was inviting even to the nervous, quick-flying birds of the air. And we think of Albert Schweitzer, who gave up a life of fame and comfort in Europe to minister to the poor, sick, and hurt of the African rain forest. In our mind's eye we see Schweitzer's gnarled, but still talented fingers, drumming out a silent chorale on the rough boards of his dining table.

When Jesus went about doing good, by his example he set free the spirit of goodness in millions of men and women, and he can do it in us.

A great divinity school once had several outstanding theologians on its faculty. Some of these men were much more "orthodox" than others. In particular, one teacher was extremely well versed in the New Testament and devoutly confessed the creeds of the church. Just across the hall from this professor's office was the study of another theologian. This second man had ideas of his own, some of them considered heretical by the students and faculty. Nevertheless, the unorthodox teacher was kind and generous; he was helpful and concerned about his students far beyond any teacher's call of duty. And over the years a saying arose among the students of this school: "If you want to know what Jesus Christ *means*, go *ask* the orthodox theologian; but if you want to know what Jesus Christ *does*, go *watch* the unorthodox one."

In his life, despite his teaching, the unorthodox teacher revealed the kind of Savior Jesus Christ is. And most of us, quite properly, are more concerned with deeds than with words.

One Marine veteran of the terrible winter of 1950 in North Korea remembers the chaplain, a Roman Catholic, and how the men loved him. He could have preached to them on their general sinfulness, and been theologically and realistically correct; instead, he usually preached words of comfort to the frightened and fatigued men. In this way, the chaplain met their needs and kept their morale high.

Jesus, when "he went about doing good," was concerned with justice for all, interested in others' happiness and personal fulfillment. He showed by his actions that God loves the children he has created, despite their tendency to stray from his ways. Jesus showed it by giving his love to the people he met, especially to the unlovable.

And we must do the same. By the power of the living Christ Jesus who dwells in our hearts, we can manifest the same genuine concern for other people in their real needs. To be truly Christians, we must do this. By the power of the selfsame Spirit that was in Jesus Christ, we can. And thus we can help to overcome the hurts in our lives and in the lives of others.

We can see that going about doing good is something somewhat different from what we previously thought. Indeed, as we've seen, trying to do good to other people when they don't want it, or in a way that is really a wrong-headed idea of our own, can do more hurt than good. But truly doing good, authentically meeting people in their needs, actually doing for them what they would like to have done, that is doing good; that is being a healing follower of a healing Christ.

Older religious visions spoke much of blessedness, the happiness that comes to the Christian from living in union with Christ. In medieval times, much was said of the vision of God. After the Reformation, among the Reformed and Lutheran theologians, much was written of union with Christ. All of these terms really apply to becoming coinheritors of the kingdom with Christ, and of becoming co-workers with him in the healing work that the church does on earth. To be a coinheritor with Christ is to join him as a fellow believer in God and to join him as a fellow healer. It also means that we will do good. It means that we will achieve our maturity as Christians and as human beings, not by seeking our own healing, only, but by seeking it in conjunction with and cooperation with all the others, great and small, who love Christ.

To reach the blessedness of union with Christ is not to fall into some sort of mindless, shallow triumphalism or joy; it is not to fall into some other-worldliness that simply says that the problems of this world and this life are not important. Rather, it means to be delivered from the immobilizing power of fear and anxiety. It means to be delivered by Christ—to be saved by him—from the kind of fearfulness that grows out of too tender feelings for the self, that grows out of selfishness and short-sightedness.

To have union with Christ and to reach blessedness does not mean that we will not continue to hurt and to have hurts, and perhaps even to encounter more hurts than we did before; Martin Luther recognized that his troubles began when he became a Christian. When we take on other people's concerns, when we begin to look at their happiness and their wholeness and at the wholeness and healthiness of society, and not think just of ourselves, there is so much more room for hurt and harm to come to us. But we do have deliverance in salvation, we do have the ability to live in courage and faith. This is the achievement of maturity. It is true integration of personality, true transcendence, true religious joy, the achievement of faith and courage. It is not our own achievement but a plateau, a high place or high plains in life to which we are brought by Jesus' power.

To have courage and not to be afraid is to be above and beyond the real hurts of life—to be beyond the power of sin and death, and the devil and the law. But it is not to be without hurt. It is to be free for growth, growth in the dangerous spaces, growth in the hard past, growth in the difficulties of life. Joy is ours on the open field of battle, as well as in the coziness of our front rooms. This is the healing power of Christ and the only way hurt can be overcome, through learning to choose the tough, yet nourishing meat of the Word, and to do away with the need for the milk of the Word, to stop being children and to start being men and women.

Maturity

Overcoming hurt in life is largely a question of maturation, and maturation is a question of integration of all the various elements of a personality. Much of the hurt we feel in life and produce in others is probably caused by our failure to recognize the various dynamics that make up our identity. We are unaware of the many dimensions of life. When we become aware of some of the dimensions that we do not care to develop, we are often ashamed of those dimensions or attempt to repress them. Maturity and a desire to put oneself together in a functioning way comes when we learn that we must accept all that there is about ourselves. This is quite difficult for anyone to do. Sometimes when a minister suggests such realism a lay person is shocked. It's so natural to deny elements in our personalities or in our lives by simply pushing them away or giving them a negative valuation. We almost come to believe that this denial is the Christian way to deal with things.

It comes as a shock to see that Christianity does not teach us to deal with the elements in our life, even those elements which are demonic, by repressing or pushing them away. Rather, Christianity, with its strong teaching about sin, and its recognition of the imperfection of everyone, teaches us that we deal with every element in our lives, all of the dimensions of life, by forgiveness. This is quite different from denial. To accept ourselves for what we are, by the power of God and with the aid of our loved ones and friends, takes courage. Courage has been summed up by someone who said that he had died with Christ and conse-

146

quently he is a dead person now, on furlough. There is no longer anything to fear, after we have passed through the trauma of recognizing our shortcomings and offering them up to God. In forgiveness we forgive and forget, and we take back the life that has been given us as a gift from God. Since it is no longer ours alone, we need not fear losing it. We can learn to live with courage. For courage is, at bottom, the ability to forget ourselves and to lose ourselves in some larger project or purpose.

Sometimes men and women who do this lose themselves in their love, and therefore they have courage to protect their families. At other times in history we have seen noble men and women who have forgotten themselves and their own interests and lost themselves in the interest of their country or their community. They have even died to protect the state or their city. For the Christian to lose himself in God, to look at himself in the harsh light of reality, with all his hurts, and with all his sins, yet to offer that up to God, and to take it back again as a gift, is to lose himself then in the larger work of God's kingdom. One can then begin to live with courage.

What does courage mean in terms of psychological problems and social relations? It means not being ashamed, not being backward or timid. Courage means being able to face everything and talk about everything. It means not having to prove anything any longer; it means being open. But of course, the more open and willing we are to talk, the more possibilities there are for other people, who are not as open or as forgiving as we are, to hurt us. We have to take that risk. All kinds of courage, physical and moral, involve risk-taking.

Part of the risk involved in the courage of accepting our life back from God might be the risk of undergoing counseling, or even therapy, if the hurts that trouble us are deep and strong enough. Courage certainly will mean taking the risk of trusting someone else when there are problems in life that do not seem to be resolving themselves, by themselves. It would mean taking the risk of trusting your pastor or asking advice and processing all of your problems with him. It would mean risking psychotherapy or psychological counseling if the problems that confront us are deep enough to warrant that kind of treatment. It involves the courage to accept whatever is necessary to work through problems that may be disturbing us—or our family or friends.

There is a healing power, then, when we are willing to accept help from others. This healing comes both from the resources of wisdom and love that these human beings might have, but also from the love and wisdom that flows through them from God. Counseling in this sense can be a sacrament. It can be the visible means of an invisible grace by which God imparts healing through sessions that we have with one another. Here is trust and faith—here is where courage and risk-taking can pay dividends. Hurts can begin to hurt less. Just as a sprain slowly begins to put itself right again, and slowly we are able to put weight on an ankle that has been turned, even the worst hurt slowly can lose its soreness and the bitterness of pain, and we can begin again to put weight on the broken bones of life together.

Hope, Fear, and Courage

Fear is a terrible form of hurt. Nothing is so cruel as fear. Only one thing can overcome the fears that grip us and depress us. That is the hope that comes with faith in Christ.

Notice that I have said *hope*. Hope, I maintain, is the opposite of fear. Most people think courage is fear's opposite. It is hope and fear that struggle together within people's emotions, not fear and courage. In the New Testament, we read "perfect love casts out fear," and that's true of a slavish fear of God. Yet Christians retain fears and worries; they do not become perfect people in any respect (even in love) when they become Christians. But Christians can grow in Christian hope.

As long ago as the time of Socrates (fourth century before Christ), men knew that hope is the opposite of, the antidote to, fear. Plato reports a conversation between Socrates and a famous Greek general, Laches, in a dialogue entitled *Laches*. Socrates was himself a war hero. He had received a standing ovation from the Athenian Senate on two occasions for his combat accomplishments as a common soldier. This was the Greek equivalent of our Congressional Medal of Honor. But Socrates was no "blood and guts" militarist. The philosopher valued peace and reasonableness. He despised phoniness and loved to disclose, by question and answer, the false ways in which people used language. In *Laches*, Socrates explains to the old general why it is a misuse of language to make fear and courage opposites. The general took the usual position that courage is the opposite of fear. He felt that a soldier loses his fear when he musters his courage to fight. What the officer must do is to stir up in the soldiers the will to close, physically, with the enemy—to carry the battle to the other side and inflict injury upon the opposing party.

Wise old Socrates, who had seen more than his share of combat in two wars, said things aren't that simple. When a soldier has no fear he isn't courageous. He is simply ignorant. A man without some fear is not a normal man. A soldier with no fear is dangerous to those who serve with him. An intelligent man in battle knows the dangers that face him. Naturally, humanly, the person engaged in conflict is afraid. Only an insensitive person of low intelligence can face an armed enemy and the possibility of injury and death without some feeling of terror.

A person without fear may appear courageous, at first, and even have a small edge on his more frightened colleagues. But, in the long run, his ignorance will prove disastrous. This falsely courageous man will take needless risks and may lose a battle because of his lack of precaution.

Socrates concludes that courage is more than lack of fear. Courage, rather, is the knowledge of what we should fear and of appropriate responses to such challenges. One should know the risk he is taking in trying to do anything— to win a battle or to overcome unhappiness or human hurt. Socrates said that courage means the acceptance of risk, then confidently going through with our task. Fear does not destroy the courageous man. He goes on with his business in faith, in hope. On what does he ground his hope? For the Christian, the answer is—on God.

Later philosophers and theologians developed Socrates' ideas on courage more fully. Paul Tillich wrote an important book, *The Courage to Be*,[2] on just this topic. Tillich's book has helped many people. You may want to read it.

Paul Tillich belonged to the generation who suffered through World War I. He saw Hitler climb to power in post-World War I Germany and sought to oppose him. Tillich was forced to flee his homeland and come to America. Like many thoughtful people, then and now, he felt that the modern world, the world of our history, was a bit insane. The events which nations provoked seemed meaningless and stupid. What do you say to a culture that has two World Wars? That burned six million Jews and killed millions of others in death camps? That dropped atomic bombs on cities? Man seems enmeshed in a whirlpool of meaninglessness. This is an awful spiritual state in which to be.

What can mankind do? Tillich responded, man can look at the senselessness and meaninglessness around him and shout out: "I am a person. Yes, a person. *I* have meaning and purpose. Stupid as the world about me may seem, *I* will affirm that *I* have meaning."

Tillich was not writing from an ivory tower. He was in the front lines for four years in World War I. His was the first name Hitler wrote on his death list when he took power in Germany in 1933. Tillich had stood up and affirmed meaning.

Tillich called this kind of courage, the courage to be. That it, it is the courage to say *you* have meaning and purpose in a mindless world. We know that we can muster this kind of courage, even when we are afraid, because we have hope—hope based on our faith in Jesus Christ, who has come to give meaning to life, the more abundant life of eternity.

Today the medical profession, the psychological profession, and the various psychotherapies and other treatments are well developed in our country. There are many ways and many techniques by which we can be helped, even with our most deep-seated problems. Many of these techniques involve the use of medication. We know that until comparatively recent times, the state asylums were full of people who had problems that did not seem to allow their going home again. But after the advent of certain drugs and treatments based on them, the asylums have been largely de-populated and people have returned to their communities again where their problems can be handled by the proper use of these drugs. Now these are great blessings and we must think that God sends them. But we must warn against dependence upon drugs. We want to warn, also, that the only proper way of taking medication or using drugs for the alleviation of hurt is under the guidance of a fully licensed physician. Many times we suffer unnecessarily or cause a burden on our families because we are not receiving available medications that might correct our problems. At other times, we are on medications, but we come to believe that we can stand alone without those medications and then we fall back into the errors which caused our problems in the first place.

I'm thinking of a young man, a minister of the Gospel, a very fine person with whom I became acquainted. Ed had suffered, perhaps since his childhood, from a severe mental disorder. His problem had been regulated and kept under control by the use of medication. As long as Ed took his medication, he had no problems at all, but from time to time he would fall under the influence of fellow Christians who felt that he could be healed by faith, no longer requiring medication. Whenever he discontinued his medication, Ed would slip back into the kind of depression and warped thinking that characterized his illness and would cause himself a great deal of pain and his friends a great deal of embarrassment. I do not want to imply that taking drugs is always wrong. I simply want to point out the tendency in our culture to be overly dependent upon drugs and to say that we shouldn't ask for drugs or seek them out. But when drugs and medications are prescribed for us by proper physicians, we should take them devoutly, knowing that God works through means and that these are the means in this case by which he will bring his healing to bear upon us.

From time to time we read stories about entertainers, writers, or people in the mass media who burn themselves out from taking pills. Unfortunately, this kind of pill addiction is fairly widespread in our society. When I was a university professor, I saw many college-age students who had already taken this destructive route. There are mood energizers and there are depressants. The students sometimes called them "uppers" and "downers." The energizers or uppers give us more pep, make us optimistic, and elevate our feelings. The depressants or downers tend to have the opposite effect, to calm us down and cool us off. Now these kinds of drugs are quite valuable in the hands of the trained physician. They can be used to give us temporary or continuous relief from problems of a severe or disabling nature. But in the hands of someone who is taking them for "kicks," or who simply wants to experiment, these pills are deadly.

We have enough hurts in our lives without taking on these artificial hurts. Life will bring us enough problems without our poisoning ourselves in this way. There is no doubt that this misuse of drugs and abuse of medication is even more dangerous than the use of alcohol. Alcohol should not be written off as just a minor problem. It is the most frequently abused drug and should be considered such. Alcohol abuse can denote a disease which can't be treated just by calling it a sin. The use of all kinds of drugs, in an abusing way, leads only to more and more hurt.

Very often, our hurts take the form of depression, which we have discussed earlier in this book. It is true that alcohol tends to have a positive effect on depression, at least in some stages. Liquor can, temporarily, relieve that depressed feeling and consequently, one can become addicted to alcohol. But over the longer haul, alcohol is itself a depressant and only complicates our problems. We hurt too much to drown our sorrow. Our only healing lies in forgiveness and insight.

Perhaps enough is not said about the healing power of friendship. I've alluded to this in talking about counseling as the possibility of sitting with someone and receiving the love of God through that person's personality. Phillips Brooks, the great preacher, once observed that preaching was truth plus personality. Counseling for the Christian is certainly God's power plus the human personality of the counselor. But one need not be a professional counselor or minister to be a little Christ to his neighbor. One can be a friend, and that includes a great deal more than being an acquaintance or speaking to someone kindly. A friend is one who shares one's troubles as well as his joys. We might think about the possibility of turning to our friends when we are "down" or have hurts and problems. Many times, of course, people do this. It's a practice among housewives to visit one another and talk over problems. For men, however, this sharing is sometimes more difficult. That man is very fortunate who has someone with whom he can open himself. He knows that his friend will not take advantage of the knowledge of his hurts and problems on the job. It's great if a man has someone to whom he can talk frankly. How necessary it is for both sexes to have someone to talk to about the things that hurt them.

We might observe that a true friend is someone who helps us to complete ourselves. And we are a true friend to others when we help them to complete themselves. Oftentimes, we really don't want to invest the energy and the time involved in being a true friend—or the trust required in allowing someone else to be our friend. A great deal of the hurt in the world might never happen, or might easily be overcome, if we were more open to friendship. This is something to think about. It is something to consider as we plan our social lives.

In our culture great stress is placed on independence. Interdependence, while certainly much more realistic and closer to what actually exists in life, is not thought to be of the same value as independence. Some years ago an American poet wrote a poem entitled, "Declaration of Interdependence." This is precisely what I'm talking about here.

To become a friend we must in some way cultivate the spirit of gentleness. This doesn't mean sloppy sentimentality, being simply plastic, bending with everything. Gentleness means not being judgmental, not casting stones. It means not putting people down, and not being defensive. Gentleness means being open and tolerant and listening. It means support, not judgment. We judge ourselves harshly enough; we do not really need the judgment of others. We need support and gentleness. A person need not condone anything that we do, if he will only listen to us. So often the only possible way for us to overcome a hurt, be it physical or mental, is for time to pass and for rest to be experienced. And the gentility of friendship, with its willingness to talk or to listen, or simply to be silent, is the equivalent, in the case of a hurt feeling, to the rest in bed we take when we hurt one of our limbs. Gentleness is important; gentleness is love and wisdom brought to bear upon our hurt.

Being a friend is not easy. So if we are willing to be someone's friend only so long as he doesn't hurt our feelings, we will never really be a friend. Friends are not acquaintances who avoid harsh issues, or avoid controversy with one another. Friends are not those who are friends only so long as personal philosophies are identical with both persons. A friend is not one who turns away when the problem gets so large in the other person's life it might tend to involve him as well. The old saying, "A friend in need is a friend indeed," is genuinely true. Perhaps we don't know who our friends are until we are in desperate need and we see the few, the very few people who stand with us, and are willing to talk with us and to talk for us, and to help us. All the many friends we thought we had may turn out to be just acquaintances, just people who had similar ideas. But a friend is like God in this respect, in that God loves us in spite of what he knows we are. And a friend loves us in spite of what he knows we are. This is a true friend and a friend who does not desert us.

Talking with a friend or a loved one, is good, but more than talk is needed. Often silence is the finest medicine a friend can bring to bear upon our hurts. Just to be with someone, to be silently standing by, is a healing thing. In my pastoral and counseling experience, I've dealt with death and funerals many times. Often in such cases it is best to do or say nothing, but just to be present, to be in silent prayer, and to be supportive by sitting beside a person. We do not need to talk about everything. In fact, many things cannot be talked about for there are no words to express some of our deepest feelings.

Finally, the identification of friendship, of being a friend, or having a friend as part of the way of overcoming hurt, does merge into the whole question of being interdependent and being happy about it. Interdependency merges into gentleness. When we are not interdependent, when we are not closely connected to each other, we might be able to be less gentle, or louder, but when we are working in close relationship, when we are working in a close dependence with someone, the gentility of manners is needed to keep down friction. Good manners can sometimes be a facade to conceal emptiness within. But genuine good manners flow out of gentleness and concern for others in the group. In this way balm is applied to many of the hurts of life.

Amazingly, after all is said about the horrors of war (horrors which are real and far more brutal than can ever be communicated through any media), many people still remember the wars that they fought in as the high points of their lives. When you talk to them, you find out they point to the interdependency, to the relationships they had with a few good friends. The kind of dependency that builds up among the members of an aircraft crew, sailors on the same ship, and soldiers in the same platoon, are friendships deeper perhaps and more real than any they have known before, or known since, in civilian life. These dependencies, for they are dependencies as well as friendships, are of the ultimate kind. One simply must be able to depend upon the other fellow when life and death can turn upon personal responsibility. One must be able to talk or not talk about anything, when you live together, under each other's noses, months on end, year after year. There must be a tolerance, a live-and-let-live attitude, a forgiving attitude, or else life is not possible together. Why can't we have these kinds of dependencies, these kinds of friendships, these kinds of gentlenesses, in the everyday work of peace? Why can't we be willing to rely upon others and be willing to let them rely upon us, in the same way that men in a combat unit must rely upon each other? Is it only crisis that can bring out the best responses in people?

So much of our society is based upon taking advantage of

others, using them, manipulating them, that many of us are afraid of being taken advantage of, are afraid of being manipulated to the point that we cannot really be friends with one another. We think "use" is a bad word; to be used is a bad thing. And yet if we are not willing to be used, not willing to use others, how can we accomplish anything in this world, for ourselves, or for other people? No one lives or dies alone. The willingness to enter into cooperative effort. with one another, not to be used as a means, but to be used as an end, a purpose in ourselves, is part of civilized society. A friend who will not remain a friend because he feels taken advantage of, is not really a friend. And if we are afraid to be friends with others because we might be imposed upon, then we're not truly willing to be friends. Friendship is take and give, and it is quite as much give as it is take. True friendship does not keep score. I do not simply repay a favor by feeling that I owe you a meal and I must ask you over. Friendship is more than that. It is based on need and on genuine liking—on what we might call love. So much of the hurt of the world would be gone if we knew truly how to be friends.

Finally, we must realize the truth of what Jesus says in the Sermon the Mount: "Blessed are the meek, for they shall inherit the earth" (Matt. 5:5). The meek are the gentle of this world. They are those who endure—those who continually strive to give and to take, and who never judge, who are not selfish. Meekness does not mean timidity or cowardice. We read in the Old Testament that Moses was very meek, but we also read that he was brave and outspoken. He was meek because he could give and take; he could use and he could be used. He was meek only after he stopped trying to put the task to which God called him on his brother and others. The meek are those who are the instruments of God. We may be called to meekness. You and I may be hurt and hurting terribly because we lack meekness. Maybe some of the hurt we feel is a misplaced hurt, a hurt that should not really be a hurt at all, but simply be the sign that we are being used for God's purposes. Perhaps we ought to look again at meekness.

Overcoming hurt is something that can occur in this life. It is too easy to say that time heals all hurts. Some hurts do respond well to the passage of time. The most severe grief, when worked through after some time has elapsed, no longer hurts the way it once did. But there are many, many other forms of hurt that are less dramatic than grief, or separation, or loss. These do not respond well to the passage of time, but simply hurt more as the years pass and we do not deal with them. One of the things I would like to get across is that hurts will not necessarily go away or get better if we simply deny them. It is far better to bring hurts out in the open and deal with them. The truth, we are told, will make us free, but the truth is something that is brought out in the light of day, that is looked at openly. People who do the truth work in the daytime and their deeds are exposed openly. To overcome hurt we must have the courage to take these kinds of risks and to talk about what really hurts us.

It is difficult to be this free and open in exposing one's self. Everything in our society tells us to protect ourselves, to keep quiet, not to show our hand. But this goes directly counter to honesty and openness, to interdependency and friendship. This is not the way in which we can deal adequately with our hurts. We must bring them to Jesus Christ, who is the Helper and who can aid us with every hurt.

Think of this power of Christ's healing and Christian maturity as acting in concert with each other. We need to grow up into Christ, who is the head, as the Bible puts it. Paul tells us that Christ learned obedience, that he became obedient, that he put aside his glory and honor, and took upon himself the form of a servant. Jesus was willing to suffer, to suffer even the death on a cross. This, too, is part of putting on Christ. We must avoid triumphalism, a sense of easy victory, the kind of cheap grace that Dietrich Bonhoeffer denounced. We cannot come to the full achievement of Christian maturity simply by saying that we believe in Christ and by acting "Christian" in some exterior way. There must be an inner growth. And just as Christ first had to descend, first had to humble himself and to learn obedience and to become a suffering servant, even so we, too, must suffer. We must know hurt, pain, and anxiety, in order that we, too, might grow up and become more godly, and more humane. The integration of personality, the bringing together of all the aspects of life can come only through this process of healing and growing. In this sense, we might say that God brings good out of evil to our lives and to the life of the world. He can make hurts to be stepping stones to higher elevations of character, to greater insights, to more thoughtful love. He can restore us, not just to what we once were, but he can restore us to wholeness and make us *more* than we ever were, because we have grown, even through our shortcomings. There is a happiness that lies beyond hurt, as we will see, but this happiness lies in growth, in fulfillment; it lies in what we can be— more like Christ—in his suffering and in his triumph over it.

This may sound like sheer wishful thinking to someone who has not plumbed the depths of his own hurt, nor been aware of the power there is in Christ and known the character that faith can give men and women. I know a couple, both of whom had disastrous first marriages. There was a great deal of hurt and turmoil and there were children involved in both cases. But both of these people tried to learn through what they had suffered; both of them returned to the church; both of them tried to grope after a way of growth. Both of them were highly responsible with regard to their children. Eventually, they found each other and a second marriage took place. Now that marriage is growing and those children are blessed by it. With all the complications in their lives because of child custody orders and visits back and forth, there is a growth and an openness and happiness. This would not be there if they did not have the history they have, nor the faith.

Zwingli, the famous Protestant reformer in Switzerland, was a priest in the medieval Catholic Church. He was a great intellect, but he was profoundly melancholy, not able to bear the duties of the priesthood. He fell into gross sin, and at one point he lay severely ill. Many thought he was on his deathbed. At this point he underwent a dramatic conversion and became a Protestant. After this his life changed. He had always loved music. Playing musical instruments became his trademark. He was thereafter famous for joy and for courage, which he found in his faith. Some people attacked Zwingli and his reforms because of his life before his conversion. But they missed the point. Zwingli became just what he did become because of his history. God can take even our sins and our shortcomings, even our scars and our hurts, and build his kingdom out of them. The testimony of men and women today who were lost in drug abuse and crime, and who were lifted up to a new life in Christ, tells us that God is still building his kingdom among us.

Healing Power

Life is hard. If I could suggest a universal motto for tombstones, it would be those three simple words. The vast web of technological, mechanical devices our culture has devised to shield us from the seriousness and risk of the world cannot hide that truth from one who lives for any length of time. Every Scripture, every poet, every playwright and novelist worth the name teaches us the difficulty of becoming and remaining a human being in the world. Men and women bear the brunt, not only of the blows of chance and of nature, but, most of all, the cruelties and unconcern of one another. Mankind, unlike any other species, is harder on itself than is its environment or any natural enemy. We come to birth in blood and grow into our individual identities in trauma. The path to adulthood leaves scars as well as successes on our psyches and our bodies. The philosophical concepts of good and evil are not mere abstractions of thought. They are personifications of the ambiguous conflicts within every personality and between every person and his fellowman. The yearning for healing in our time is great, but it has always been so. The ancient caves of France and India were not painted, nor the pyramids raised, nor the words of the eighth century prophets recorded because man was at peace with himself. Just the opposite—man has always felt split, between the mind and the heart, the body and the spirit, between good and evil. Therefore, mankind has always sought healing, wholeness—unity of the self with itself.

The following are only a few of the ways in which we are groping today to find this wholeness. There are no signs that the quest is diminishing.

Harry's Help

Peter Evans (a fictitious name) is a young instructor in literature. Until recently, his life has been marked by quiet despair, a deep sense of guilt, and a sense of no way out. That was before Peter met Harry. Harry is a Socratic figure, a man who goes around his city asking questions and listening to what people say. He is just far enough "out" to be real and effective in today's searching world. An executive in a large company, Harry is old enough to be the father of most of the young people he meets plying his Socratic trade. He dresses conservatively, although like Socrates he is usually rumpled and is always in conversation. His church background is Southern Baptist and his manner is warmly evangelical. However, his technique and perhaps some of his philosophy are unique to him.

Harry's similarities to Socrates lie more than just on the surface. He spends almost all his time now visiting in university areas, talking to students and their young instructors. He is highly effective in these encounters. One would think that college made people sophisticated in ways that would prevent their being affected by people like Harry, and perhaps at one time that was true. It is no longer true in this spiritually searching age. From my visits to the city where Harry resides, I would say that he is perhaps the most effective worker with young people whom I have ever met. I believe this is because Harry offers not only counsel but healing and a deep spiritual inspiration. This is what men and women are looking for today.

The search for healing is the modern version of the ancient quest, recounted in myths and legends, enshrined in our dreams. The quest is the drive of the life force within each one of us to become fully human—to actualize the full potential born within us. What are our problems and hang-ups but blocks to our self-actualization? Who are our enemies if not the immature parts of our own selves? The search for healing is the unconscious urge to reunite the unconscious and the conscious minds, to make the stuff of dreams and the elements of reality one.

Harry is the improbable countercultural hero of today's spiritual search because he represents a living combination of traditional religious attitudes and an openness to what we have traditionally thought of as occult interests. He takes seriously the reality of spirits and demons, and he is himself a practicing psychic. Harry is at ease in the informal relationships and the language of astrology that forms so much of the behavior and speech of young people today. He seems like a person programed to seek out and zero in on spiritual needs. Harry uses a natural psychic ability to attract people's attention and to close in on them with his "preaching." In the case of Peter Evans, he sensed the distress in the man and was used of God to bring about a profound conversion which appears to have made both Peter and his wife very happy. While this may seem somewhat like ordinary evangelism, it is hardly that. Harry introduced Peter and his wife to another professor, Jim, and Jim's wife. They all entered a world where spiritual things were more real than the concrete events of everyday. Through these four young adults Harry's circle is now reaching the students in the large university where they teach. A spiritual group has sprung up in the home of one of them that has attracted students who previously had no connection with the church.

The thrust of this story is that it is possible to overcome hurt, by the power of the Risen Lord, Jesus Christ, which is released in our lives through faith. We may feel that life is meaningless and full of despair and suffering before we come to such a faith in Christ. Indeed, we are correct if we think that life is meaningless apart from a lively faith in God through Christ. Facing the world on our own, with the resources of our own mind and bodies only, it is natural that we should fail and fall. Apart from participation in the community of faith, the living body of Christ, the church fellowship, is no more than a word. It is natural that we would feel lonely and fearful. Theologically, such a situation can be correctly termed "living in sin," although our lives may be quite ethical. The point is that our lives are meaningless and have no purpose without Christ. In such a state everything can and does hurt us. When faith enters our lives we are still subject to the accidents of the world and the effects of sin, but we have a healer. To live by faith is to live in a manner that means we are on the way to overcoming hurt.

As David Seabury observed in his book, *How Jesus Heals Our Minds Today:*

Modern psychologists have not been able to add to the

philosophy of Jesus but, restating it in modern terminology, have shown how deeply he recognized the principles of personal fulfillment. Today as never before we understand the parable of the talents. We know, all too well, the price of inertia and inactivity. We have seen in clinic and in consultation room what happens to bodies that become torpid, senses dulled almost to anaesthesia and minds grown befogged and dull from lack of use.

From the new psychology we have learned that there are two types of people. We call them active and passive personalities, givers and receivers, participants and spectators, or in the New Testament terms, doers and hearers. Whichever term one prefers, we all recognize the individual who is moving forward, concerned with self-expansion, developing his capacities to the utmost, seeking varied avenues of expression, giving himself wholly to each undertaking. Whatever his personal fortunes he is able to experience joy, for he is in touch with the deeper springs of his nature and aware of the great fellowship of those who with him are moving toward an ever greater fulfillment. This is the road that leads to health and to that peace of God which passeth understanding.

The way of one who is vegetative and inert is in the direction of negation, torpor, sickness, and personal extinction. People of this kind are held back by fear, crystallized into rigid grooves by slavery to social patterns, niggardly with their spiritual resources. Such individuals, egocentric either from neurosis or selfishness, never become instruments of their greater capacities, because their motion is toward themselves and away from life. Those without zest, who live as spectators only, gradually die on their feet. They walk among us as phantoms, for they do not know that only by spending themselves generously can they be sustained.

If you make a quick census of your acquaintances, how many can you count who are living up to their capacity? Some, of course, you find concentrated upon a single, personal goal, particularly if they are driven by ambition or possessed of a special ability. Most of us, however, live with our brakes on. It is the fashion to think of Americans as speeded up to a pitch of nervous tension unknown in other countries. But this jerky, jazzy existence, with its dozens of unrelated activities, is not the life more abundant pictured by Jesus. If it were, we should not hear so much about fatigue and nervous breakdown, with their attendant physical deterioration. Have you noted that in the work of Jesus there is no record of time out for sickness? [3]

Let us follow Seabury's advice and elect to follow Jesus who gives the power to live beyond fatigue and anxiety and let the hurts go.

Happiness Beyond Hurt

Happiness Beyond Hurt

5

Marriage is not so light a state that it can be entered into without thought and dissolved without pain. God joins us together in a manner that is like the grafting of flesh on flesh. Man's law cannot undo that joining without trauma and the cutting into of living tissue.

In Genesis 2:18–24, there is the lovely account of the creation of Eve for Adam. Eve, the Bible tells us, was formed from the very material of Adam's body. Adam and Eve, the man and the woman, are one flesh. The upshot is that God ordains and blesses marriage. As the commentary written into the text says, men and women are to leave their parents and stand by one another for a lifetime. God intends that people stay together in the marriage relationship.

Jesus underscored all this in the famous passage in Mark 10:2–16. At that place, under the questioning of skeptics, Jesus declared that the Hebrew practice of divorce was the result of a hardness of heart. Divorce may have been legal, but it did not represent the will of God.

On the basis of this and similar passages, some churches have held that divorce is absolutely forbidden for the Christian. It is certainly true that divorce is not to be encouraged, but such an absolute prohibition can lead to greater unhappiness than the results of divorce itself. It also rests on a deep misunderstanding of the message of the Bible. That message is that all people are sinful. We are sinful whether we are single, married, or divorced. The outcome of divorcing one another may be adultery, but Jesus also tells us in another place that adultery is the result of thinking erotically about someone else (Matt. 6:28). This well-known point of Christian ethics, unfortunately misunderstood, became an issue for a time in the 1976 presidential election, when Jimmy Carter granted his now-famous interview with *Playboy* magazine.

The intent of Jesus' discussion in Mark 10 is to show that Christianity recognizes the common sinfulness of everyone of us. The fact that we are sinners is the very reason Christ came to earth, to achieve the forgiveness of our sins, by his sacrifice on the cross.

The fact of sin cannot be stressed enough, when we consider the nature of human happiness and the unhappiness so common in our generation, as in every other. In a perfect world, where people were perfect, there would be no sin, and there would be no unhappiness. But this is not a perfect world; it is one characterized by the fall of man. It is a world in which, as St. Augustine wrote in the fifth century, A.D., it is impossible for us not to sin.

Yet we are not to glory in sin, or to think that we can sin so that grace may come. Grace is not cheap. Forgiveness is not free, although it is freely given to us. Forgiveness cost the life of Jesus and it is the constant work of the Spirit in the Christian church. But having said all this, it remains true that there are no sins that cannot be forgiven, not even divorce, except the sin of denying that forgiveness is possible. This denial of forgiveness is an ultimate negativism, a choosing of unhappiness that the Bible calls sin against the Holy Spirit.

For those who are willing to accept their sinfulness, recognizing their own limitations and shortcomings, there is the possibility of finding happiness beyond hurt. Such an acceptance is the situation that the theologian, Paul Tillich, calls accepting our acceptance. It means coming to terms with our own feelings of anxiety and despair, our own sense of inferiority and indecision, and letting them go because we have faith that God accepts us in spite of all these failures. We must go one step beyond, however, to the acceptance of the limitations and shortcomings of others, without passing negative judgments upon them. Once we accept our own imperfection and that of the other person, the possibility of happiness becomes real. Even in lives marred by years of strife, there is the potential for peace and cooperation when we surrender images of perfection that none of us ever achieve. Coming to terms with the sinful self is part of accepting the forgiveness of God and entering the path that leads to happiness beyond hurt.

Laugh and the World Laughs with You

We have all heard the proverb, "Laugh and the world laughs with you, cry and you cry alone." While many old sayings aren't necessarily always true, this one comes close to universal truth. As human beings, we are drawn to laughter and happiness, and we are naturally repelled by tears and unhappiness.

Happiness makes us feel warm inside, safe, secure. Happiness gives us good feelings all through our bodies. Unhappiness is a negative state of being. It makes us feel bad, depressed.

The famous Russian novelist and Christian thinker, Count Leo Tolstoy, observed that happy children are very much alike, wherever they live in the world. Happiness is a universal emotion. But Tolstoy also noticed that unhappy children aren't alike. Each unhappy child has his own particular form of unhappiness. Unlike happiness, crying and unhappiness have unique qualities with each separate person. Happiness, then, unites us. Unhappiness divides and separates us from one another.

Happiness As Forgiven-ness

Once we have surrendered the unconscious images of perfection that keep us passing negative judgments on others and either feeling inferior, or else defensively protesting our own perfection, then we can begin life as a process of daily forgiveness. Paradoxically, we find that we will accomplish more good when we expect less than we do when we hold impossible standards up to ourselves and others. Yet this is easy to say and far harder to put into practice. Living by forgiveness is simple, but not easy. It is precisely as simple, and exactly as easy, as casting our cares on Christ.

Too many times we are told to cast our cares on Christ as if it were an easy thing to do. We find ourselves in the position of the cold and hungry Christians mentioned in the Epistle of James. Those poor people were told to go in peace and be warmed and fed (James 2:14–17). That's easy to say and not so easy to do. It is not easy for a human being to let go, to stop cherishing his secret sins, to stop defending himself against all comers. Yet it is precisely such a letting-go that is needed before Christ can come into one's life. It is not that we must clean ourselves up and get ourselves all perfect before Christ will have anything to do with us. To the contrary, it is only when we acknowledge our lack of goodness and our lost condition that Christ can make a difference in our lives. This was the experience of St. Augustine, Martin Luther, John Wesley, and John Bunyan.

Happiness beyond hurt is not a thing, a state, a condition—it is a process. Happiness is never an absolute achievement, but it is the result of a way of life, the life of a

172

forgiven sinner, the by-product of a life of faith that ushers in love.

Once we think of happiness as a way of life, as a by-product that comes to us uninvited, we see that happiness is always a gift. C. S. Lewis speaks of the happiness of the Christian life as being "surprised by joy." This is the case. Happiness is that which takes hold of us when we do not seek it and least expect it.

If we can understand these truths about happiness then our knowledge is good, but we do not necessarily *have* what we understand. Happiness is not something that can be learned. It can only be experienced. Now we turn to an examination of some of the elements of that experience.

It is much too easy to offer pat answers, religious or psychological, designed to fit everyone. Like shoes designed to fit all people, such answers fit no one in particular. Just as there are no average people, there are no average problems and no average solutions. There are no average religious questions and no average religious answers. Ultimately, pious generalities cannot help us since we can only hear answers to questions which we ask ourselves. If something is amiss in our lives, it may be similar to the problem of someone else, but it is never precisely the same.

To talk intelligently about living by forgiveness, we must understand that such a process involves maturity. Our culture is a shallow one that equates happiness with a good time and good times with the sensual aspects of life. For this reason, youth is looked upon as the genuinely happy time of life. We are surprised when we turn to the writings of the wise and find that the proverbs of the Old Testament and the writings of the philosopher, Aristotle, on happiness, both equate the achievement of a happy life with age.

Aristotle believed that it was impossible for a person to be happy unless he had lived a long life. So convinced was he that maturity, what psychologists today call integrity, was essential to the achievement of happiness that he wrote, "Count no man happy until you see him dead." Needless to say, our society has not generally seen old age as the ultimate in happiness.

Perhaps if we think back to our discussion of the life cycle in Chapter 1, the equation of the life of forgiveness with maturity will be clearer. It is part of the psychology of older people to settle down, to live with decisions that have been made, and to direct their attention to a few important things. After the age of forty-four, most people turn to the development of their inner life. They pay less attention to achievements in the outer world. There is an increasing tendency to accept the way things are. This is similar to the spiritual acceptance of the self as imperfect and of others as imperfect, but yet as worthy of love.

No amount of psychological gain or therapy can make us older than we really are. It is possible that maturity, growing older and accepting it, is a major part of coming to a place where happiness can happen to us.

Many times, we may actually hurt because we haven't grown up—or at least have not become reconciled to maturity. Our pleasures may still be stuck at the pre-adult stage, where joy comes from taking, rather than from giving, which is the adult's joy. Growing up isn't easy, but maturing is even more difficult. Maturing, to me, means chiefly one thing, to come to terms with one's own limitations. In the larger framework, this means coming to terms with the fact that we must die. In the smaller frame, it means reconciling ourselves to living with the kind of person we are. No moral person can go through such a maturing process without recognizing the fact of his or her own sinfulness. This is the prelude to accepting God's acceptance, to living as a person justified by faith and not by works. Maturity, and therefore happiness, means life in forgiven-ness.

Caring

We are not only forgiven from the sin that marks us as all too human and from the actual sins of the past; we are forgiven by God to live in the present and to create the future. Faith is not opposed to good works but is the pre-condition for them. Faith leads on in the Christian life to love. Love that is not abstract but concrete and real means caring. Surprisingly, it is not cares that prevent us from being happy—it is only cares that we resent, that we really do not "care" about. Caring for others is the natural manner of life for the Christian and as such is the path that leads to the experience of happiness.

The essence of caring is to wish someone well and to be willing to work hard to bring good into that person's life. Caring is the opposite of selfishness and involves giving up goods and opportunities ourselves so that others may benefit. The most obvious model of caring is parenting. The mother and her child represent for all mankind the clearest picture of caring. No wonder the Madonna and Child picture has been the most widespread religious object in the world.

Living in forgiven-ness makes caring possible, for it is a state beyond anxiety about self, where all human energies can be directed toward the needs of the other. What happens naturally, perhaps out of instinct, and only for short periods in nourishing and protecting helpless infants, can become a steady state of living at the fully developed level of the mature adult.

Of course, living in forgiveness does not mean life in some superhuman mode—that is why forgiveness is necessary. Just as the parent, even the new mother, is not always unselfish, not always free of thoughts of herself and anxieties about herself, neither is the Christian adult. The happiness that flashes into the system of the caring person is

175

also frequently disturbed. And the disturber, even when the other is our own child, is not always loving, either. The life of forgiveness is constantly one that seeks forgiveness for the self and gives forgiveness to others. Happiness is not a steady state; only forgiveness is.

Erich Fromm, the noted psychiatrist, has produced a mammoth study on *The Anatomy of Human Destructiveness*.[1] Fromm tells us of the many ways in which the forces of destruction battle in each of us with the forces of life. That battle is the psychological dimension of sin. To live with happiness beyond hurt we must believe that we are forgiven, when we ask for it, regardless of our failures to love, and be equally believing in forgiving others for their shortcomings. This forgiveness of others must include forgetting what the other has done also.

There can be no forgiving that is not also forgetting. A life that is genuinely Christian cannot contain vengeance, and it is only the primitive desire for vengeance that makes us want to remember the bad things done to us. To err is human, to forgive divine. And to forget is to participate in the life of God, who casts our sins behind his back as far as the east is from the west.

Richard Andersen, the author of *The Love Formula*, observed:

> The doctrine of forgiveness, of God's unconditional love for us, is the core of Christianity. Yet central as forgiveness is to our faith, we often fail to live in forgiveness. We need to try in many ways to make the truth that "Christ died on the cross for our sins" take on flesh and blood reality.
>
> . . . Our actions and lives of forgiveness are the tools that most effectively teach Christianity.
>
> Forgiving and loving come especially hard when we feel threatened by people with attitudes that clash with ours. We may initially react with anger or hostility.
>
> It's important then, to understand that this initial kind of reaction is natural—perhaps even good. We must recognize

and honestly face our differences with others and our reactions to them before the differences can be resolved; and anger may be the quickest way to release pent-up emotions and get rid of disrupting tension.

However, once the anger has been released, it has served its purpose. (Maybe that's what St. Paul meant when he advised Christians of his day: "Be angry but do not sin; do not let the sun go down on your anger." Eph. 4:26.) Mature Christians will then get to the business of respecting the differences of others, confessing their own intolerance, and sharing forgiveness in the spirit of Christ, who forgave even his crucifiers.

. . . Above all, we all need help in bridging the gap of pride. Few of us like to admit we are wrong—or even give up the "right-wrong" issue and see the primary objective as building a happy relationship with our "opponent." Of course, any injustice needs to be corrected before real peace can be established. But, once we get beyond the "right-wrong" issue, we can experience the joy of forgiveness, of fellowship, of a more free-to-love way of life.

. . . At times we will be tempted to say, "That's it! I've forgiven as much and as far as I can." At those times we need to hear again the Good News that nothing can separate us (or them) from the love of God which is in Christ Jesus. Then "seventy times seven" become once again a privilege, not a chore. [2]

In his famous book, *The Irony of American History*, Reinhold Niebuhr observed:

Nothing that is worth doing can be achieved in our lifetime; therefore we must be saved by hope. Nothing which is true or beautiful or good makes sense in any immediate context of history; therefore we must be saved by faith. Nothing we do, however virtuous, can be accomplished alone; therefore we must be saved by love. No virtuous act is quite as virtuous from the standpoint of our friend or foe as it is from our own standpoint; therefore we must be saved by the final form of love, which is forgiveness. [3]

Niebuhr says it all.

Caring Is Forgiving

Among the hurts we suffer silently or shrilly in our daily lives, perhaps the most destructive are those which close us off from one another and then eat away at our vitals without relief. These are the hurts which lead to sullennesss in behavior and to ulcers and depression brought on by stress: anger, guilt, anxiety, ingratitude, and regret. Nothing hurts us more than bottled-up anger, which leads on to nervous exhaustion and frustration. Nothing is more saddening than anxiety caused by guilt and regret on our part or by ingratitude on the part of others. Like the acid such feelings produce in our stomachs, such internal conditions eat away at our lives and leave us no peace or joy.

Yet each of these conditions can be overturned in a moment by surrendering them, throwing them away, casting them on God, in an act of forgiveness. If we make the effort to forgive others, as we would wish to be forgiven ourselves, and then forgive ourselves, too, these pressures can be done away with. They can be dropped from our lives as surely as we lose a diseased organ in an operation. But we must really, genuinely forgive.

This possibility of forgiveness is the central core of the Christian message, yet it is often forgotten or only given verbal expression. True forgiveness is mind-blowing, radical, even crazy, when looked at from a worldly perspective. Consider Jesus, praying for the forgiveness of his executors while they nailed him to the cross. Consider the case of the husband who sought to pay another man to murder his wife. The man so approached went to the police, who set a trap for the murderous husband. Once the husband was arrested, the wife forgave him, then helped in his legal defense. This case took place in the United States during the 1970s. Forgiveness is world-shattering and person-building. But to rebuild persons and to turn hurt into the pathway to happiness, forgiveness must be real—a combination of faith in God and forgetfulness of any wrong done to us or by us.

Forgiving Is Not Easy

As Paul reminds us, we can know the good and not do it. The problem may be that we (and many others in history) confuse two aspects of the human will. We may confuse that aspect of the human will which we consciously control with the whole of the will. The more important part of the will is not consciously directed at all.

No one has made the matter of the will's place in human happiness clearer than Leslie H. Farber in his wise book, *Lying, Despair, Jealousy, Envy, Sex, Suicide, Drugs, and the Good Life.* [4]

Farber observes that we are happiest when our actions just flow naturally from a unity of body and mind (as in playing any sport). This subtle unity is destroyed when we begin to consciously "think" about what we're doing and try to "will" further actions. Such attempts only lead to anxiety, which Farber defines: "anxiety is that range of distress which attends willing what cannot be willed." [5]

This means that it is often fruitless to consciously will to forgive someone, or oneself. Rather, what is needed is a "forgetting," a "letting go" of conscious attachment to those feelings of hurt, rejection, anxiety, guilt, regret, and fear that the other person stirs up in us. Sometimes we tell a child, "Don't be afraid." The child answers, "I'm trying not to be afraid, but I still am." Of course, the child is still afraid. We remain in fear until we forget ourselves and enter naturally into the activities around us. Such insight is as true of adults in war as it is of children in amusement parks. We hurt until we forget, and the first thing that must be forgotten is ourselves. Yet we can't consciously *force* ourselves to forget—we can only forget!

Perhaps there's a simpler way. Whatever hurts us we can

offer up to God. We can ask him to let Christ carry it all away and consciously believe that Christ can and will until it becomes "second nature," just "natural" for us to behave that way. This we can do, although we can't do anything to help ourselves. We can have faith that God will help us.

The following strange, true story of my encounter with Alex will show just what Christ can do.

Recently Alex (a junior in a small Northern college) sat in my office and told me of the hurt he had suffered since his senior year at a large city high school. Alex was dressed neatly enough in the blue jeans and jacket of the contemporary college student. His hair was moderately long and wavy, as were his beard and mustache. Alex's story was a familiar one to anyone who has worked closely with a college community over the last decade. This young man had experimented with every kind of herb and drug. He had "done chemicals" (as the youth say) ranging from LSD-25 to mescaline. He had smoked "dope" (marijuana) frequently. At examination time, he had used "speed" (amphetamines) to stay awake and cram for his tests. Toward the end of this experimental period (for he was now "off drugs"), he had become involved with drug users of a violent disposition, who were "into" Black occultism. Their references to Satan, their fascination with guns and knives, had frightened him—quite sensibly frightened him, I think. Alex began to think of Jesus Christ and redemption from evil one morning after having a dream.

Alex fixed me with an anxious look. "Should I be talking about this?" he asked.

"Of course, if you can talk about it now and then forget about it," I answered.

"Okay, but I get upset thinking about this."

"Just don't get compulsive and think about it all the time," I rejoined.

"Well, I was smoking dope," Alex began, "and got pretty well wrecked (intoxicated) before I fell into a trance, or sleep, I'm not sure which. Anyway, I had this dream, or this vision, or this vision-in-a-dream. It was scary and comforting at the same time.

"In my dream, I was under water, floating in and out with the tide. As I would float closer in to shore, I could look down and see the clean sand below me. I could look up and see the sun's rays penetrating through the water toward me. As I approached the beach, the floor of the sea gently tilted up to meet the sandy edge, which was the edge of the ocean. The closer I came to the shore, the warmer the water became. It was quite warm and quite pleasant.

"But I also floated back out seaward. I could feel a definite pull, a kind of tidal motion. This tide made me float away from the warm water to deeper water where it was colder. At times I would feel as if I was going farther and farther out. Then I was in really deep water, so deep I could look up through many, many varied colors of water and sunlight mingled together. Once, after floating in to where it was warm, I was pulled further out than ever. I looked up and I saw a boat floating on the ocean's surface far above me. I sort of woke up and cried out, 'What is the name of this dream?' Then I saw, as it were, a television set with the words 'The Seventh Tide' displayed upon its screen. At that moment I knew that the boat was Jesus, the fisherman. He was fishing for me."

I talked with this young man for some time and I was surprised to find that he had not associated his well-developed dream with the myths and symbols of death and rebirth. The sea, the fountain of life, figured in it. The warm water with the strong in-and-out pull of the tides fairly cried out that they represented the womb and the birth process. But it was when I mentioned Paul's imagery of dying with Christ in the water of baptism and being resurrected with him as we come out of the water, that I received my biggest surprise. Alex claimed never to have read anything in the Bible, yet he was "following Jesus." He fairly trembled with joy when I gave him a New Testament. Here was one of the "Jesus people" of the purest sort. He had started "following Jesus" (his own words) without benefit of the church, the campus religious programs, the clergy, or even of the New Testament. I could not stifle the exclamation, "Out of the mouth of babes thou hast perfected praise." And a further one, "Yet wisdom is justified by all her children."

I think Jesus would have loved this boy who threw over four years of drug abuse on the strength of a vision in a drug-induced dream, without fully understanding it. Alex saw in it the one thing needful (Jesus Christ) and he saw what I did not see (Jesus as the boat) when I heard the vision recounted.

Seeing the World with Fresh Eyes

Someone has said that revelation from God is not so much the communication of information as it is God allowing us to see ourselves as we are, for the first time. And in doing that, he tells us a great deal about himself. When we come to faith, we are freed by that faith, by that healing power of Christ, to see the world with fresh eyes. It is this turn, this conversion, this "turning around" as it is in the Greek of the New Testament, *metanoia*, that is needed for us to find happiness beyond hurt. If we would begin to look at each other in our homes, factories, offices, and churches, with new eyes, full of acceptance, respect, and forgiveness for our shortcomings (and a short memory that forgets the things people have done against us), many of the problems we have as persons and in our families would disappear. To see things in a new way, to have the scales of selfishness and self-destruction, of low self-esteem and envy of others, fall from our eyes, is truly to be healed.

It is the intent of this book to stress that while Christianity may not always be the answer to every emotional and psychological problem, it is a basic part of the answer to any problem we might have. Indeed, if we were to live in this freshness of vision, in this converted state, many, if not most of the problems plaguing us and causing us hurt would never come to pass. Hurt is the result of sin. Sin is selfishness; selfishness is the refusal to forget. It is an adamant turning away from forgiveness. Often we would like to be forgiven ourselves, but we do not want to forgive others. We forget that Jesus taught us to pray, "and forgive us our trespasses, as we forgive those who trespass against us." God does give us a conditional forgiveness, and he shows us, in this prayer, that forgiveness for ourselves is conditional upon our willingness to forgive others. We cannot possess what we will not use. Forgiveness is not a document drawn up saying that we are pardoned from certain crimes; it is seeing the world with fresh eyes and ourselves for the first time clearly, and thereby seeing God and his living Christ in the world. To be alive in this new relationship of union with God through Christ is simply to go on forgiving others seventy times seventy times, over and over again, without end.

To be in Christ and to have Christ in us and to see his world anew, means that we live by morals and good manners. It is not simply a question of living by principles or codes or commandments; it is rather a question of living in accordance with the terms of the relationship that is ours. We do not do good works that good might come to us, but our tree, as it were, is a good tree in that by its nature, it must bear good fruit. The Christian does not wait to be told that he should live morally and with good manners and courtesy, and love and forgiveness, but he is already going forward in the world, doing all these things without being told.

This leads us to a life that is truly one of love—a life of harmlessness, of reverence for life. It is an absence of aggressive tendencies toward other people. The great Christian mystic of the twentieth century, Albert Schweitzer, lived such a life. In a large portion of the book he called *Reverence for Life*, Schweitzer discussed gratitude. To be reverent toward life is to be grateful for life.

To be forgiven is, indeed, to see the world with fresh eyes. It is to look upon a world newly created by Almighty God, because our spirits have been thoroughly renewed. The person who asks for God's forgiveness and accepts it, now sees that the good all wish to have instead of the hurt that plagues mankind, is nothing more or less than reverence before the life our Creator has given us. As Albert Schweitzer never tired of preaching in word and deed:

> . . . in the last resort the good consists in elemental reverence of the enigma we call life, in reverence for all its manifestations, both great and small. The good is what preserves and advances life; evil is what hinders or destroys it. We are ethical if we abandon our stubbornness, if we surrender our strangeness toward other creatures and share in the life and the suffering that surround us. Only this quality makes us men.[6]

With fresh eyes, we see that we are not separate, *apart*, but connected, *a part* of the great world of life around us. We are able to accept ourselves, as we are, and other people and creatures around us, as they are, because God, the Father, has accepted us.

As Paul Tillich tells us in his famous sermon, "To Whom Much Is Forgiven":

> He who is accepted ultimately can also accept himself. Being forgiven and being able to accept oneself are one and the same thing. No one can accept himself who does not feel that he is accepted by the power of acceptance which is greater than he, greater than his friends and counselors and psychological helpers. They may point to the power of acceptance, and it is the function of the minister to do so. But he and the others also need the power of acceptance which is greater than they. The woman in our story could never have overcome her disgust at her own being without finding this power working through Jesus, who told her with authority, "You *are* forgiven." Thus, she experienced, at least in *one* ecstatic moment of her life, the power which

reunited her with herself and gave her the possibility of loving even her own destiny.

This happened to her in one great moment. And in this she is no exception. Decisive spiritual experiences have the character of a breakthrough. In the midst of our futile attempts to make ourselves worthy, in our despair about the inescapable failure of these attempts, we are suddenly grasped by the certainty that we are forgiven, and the fire of love begins to burn. That is the greatest experience anyone can have. It may not happen often, but when it does happen, it decides and transforms everything.[7]

The Consolation of Philosophy

In looking back over a varied, full life, I have concluded that while hurt is the result of human sin, the experience of inner hurt, properly understood, is also a mark of human spirituality. If we could not feel hurt, we also could not feel happiness. Without the capacity to be injured, we would not have the ability to reach transcendence—to move beyond ourselves in identification with other people and with God. Not to feel loneliness would be the same condition as not feeling companionship and love.

The capacity to be hurt and to suffer regret because of our shortcomings also is the sure mark of the reality of our human freedom. If all were fixed, if everything were determined, we would never deviate from the plan set in motion in our lives by nature or God. We would be free of regret because we would be free of responsibility. Also, I hasten to point out, we would be moral infants, intellectual midgets, with no sense of self-hood and self-worth. There is a human sense in which we can take satisfaction in owning up to our own mistakes, for to do so means that we can find fulfillment in our equally real accomplishments. This insight is what philosophers, ancient and modern, have meant by "theodicy," the justification of the existence of evil in a world created by a righteous God. Most thinkers have agreed that the possibility of evil, of sin, of hurt, is necessary in a world that contains human freedom. Therefore, despite the hurts we suffer, all is for the best in the best of all possible worlds.

One of God's richest blessings to all human beings is that we can never remember physical pain, being hurt. We can remember the circumstances, of course, but not the actual pain itself. This is why we are able to pick ourselves up after being knocked down in a game and play hard once more.

Unfortunately, psychic or spiritual pain is somewhat different. We cannot remember the pangs of regret or the weakening effect of guilt, but in anxiety we can—and do—continue to experience the debility of emotional pain.

Christ's forgiveness can overcome this emotional distress, however. We can be freed from guilt and remorse and the anxiety they bring through faith in Jesus Christ. Dr. Morton T. Kelsey, writing of "Sharing in the Victory" of Christ in his book, *Myth, History and Faith*, speaks of some of the difficulties of the person who has just been grasped by Christ.

> How seldom do we take Jesus Christ seriously. He tells us that we are entertaining Him in our lives when we minister to the hungry, the naked, the imprisoned. And sometimes we do show love to these people, and then turn right around and cut it off from those closest to us. Again, it is not a matter of either/or, but of both/and. If we are to love others as He has loved us (a rather radical commandment, but the only really new one that He gave), it takes some real action, yes, social action, action toward helping other human beings and some real determination. Still, if we really believe that Christ, through His love, routed the forces of evil so that we could be ransomed from them, and then we don't even try to follow His way, we come close to losing ourselves in hypocrisy.

> What does this love mean? It means first of all considering the idea that, as His followers, our task is to live out love. Then it means carrying this idea out in action. It means listening to others without judging or criticizing them, because one cannot even begin to love a person until

he has at least listened and tried to find out what the other person is like. Love is not just a warm feeling towards another human being; rather, it is making the other person feel loved himself, and this is impossible without listening. It also means trying to love one's self, the most difficult of all tasks because—when we stop to think—we have the whole story on ourselves. This is one reason so few of us even try to love ourselves, and it is then impossible to love others, because we are busy projecting onto them the parts of ourselves which we cannot stand. Whenever one cannot stand some characteristic in other people, it means that that characteristic is probably unconsciously part of himself and he has not looked at it. [8]

Once we do turn our spiritual eyes, in meditation and prayer, upon every side of our personalities, we can feel the healing power of God seep through all of our selves. We can let our selves be moved on to a place of non-recrimination—a refusal to condemn or judge others—and to a life style of harmlessness, of good will toward all people, even those closest to us who may try our souls the most. As we become more benevolent toward others, in a practice of continual forgiveness and acceptance, morals and good manners, graciousness and pleasantness become our style of life. Little by little, we become the "little Christs" to our neighbors that Martin Luther preached about at the time of the Reformation. We begin to look at others to see how we can serve them, how we can heal their hurts, how we can make them happier, instead of seeing others as occasions for profits and satisfactions of our needs. Such is the world outlook of the Christ-infused personality.

The Achievement of Self-Integration

We began this study of where we hurt with a discussion of the various stages of life that human beings move through traveling toward maturity. Ultimately, the person who becomes truly mature becomes fully integrated, a firmly organized, fully functioning self. To grow up and to grow through our hurts and difficulties is to become fully self-realized.

Today there are many psychologies of self-realization that attempt to lead people to maturity without much reference to Jesus Christ. Whatever helps people to realize themselves is good, to be sure, but I feel that full maturity is achieved only when one "grows up into Christ the head" as well as in other physical and psychological respects. Long ago, St. Thomas Aquinas put it simply, "Grace does not destroy nature, but completes it." When Christ comes to us, by grace, he comes to make us more fully human and mature. In him, we find ourselves and receive the power to develop all parts of ourselves—giving us a happiness beyond anxiety, a fulfillment of life that can move through and beyond hurt.

Love Is As Strong As Death

Much of the hurt we are subject to in life is the result of the incursion of death into our lives. After all, man is a creature, one who dies and knows that he dies. Anxiety over the approach of death, ontological anxiety as Tillich has called it, pervades the human race. We may enjoy every opportunity in life, including length of days, and yet we cannot escape the last enemy, death.

Here is where Christianity stands far above every other philosophy and religion in the course of all human history. Christianity is, above all else, faith based upon the disciples' belief in Jesus Christ's victory over death. The disciples became the early Christian church because they were convinced that Jesus was resurrected from the dead.

> This Jesus, delivered up according to the definite plan and foreknowledge of God, you crucified and killed by the hands· of lawless men. But God raised him up, having loosed the pangs of death, because it was not possible for him to be held by it. . . .
>
> This Jesus God raised up, and of that we are all witnesses . . . .

The God of our fathers, glorified his servant Jesus, whom
you delivered up and denied in the presence of Pilate. . . .
and killed the Author of life, whom God raised from the
dead. To this we are witnesses (Acts 2:23, 24, 32; 3:13–15).

All this means that one who has been grasped by Christ,
who has experienced his forgiveness, has been freed from
the fear of death. It is the ultimate truth that the love of God
in Christ is stronger than death. This is the fundamental
basis of the Christian's happiness beyond hurt—the glimpse
of eternity, already experienced in time.

Our hurts all rest, ultimately, upon our finiteness, our
mortality, our limitations. Beyond us is the ability to tran-
scend time. We feel our years slipping away. It is not true
that we have lived thirty years or forty years—we have
actually been dying for thirty or forty years. We are creatures of time, just as we are subject to death. But in Christ's
love we have a sign and seal of eternity. Experiencing a
relationship that does not age or wither, we have a companionship that cannot be adversely affected by or ended even
by death. Here all hurts come into a proper perspective. We
see that nothing can finally destroy us. Nothing can prevent
our self-flowering. In the sweet taste of the eternal we come
to understand the words of Paul: ". . . nor anything else in all
creation will be able to separate us from the love of God in
Christ Jesus our Lord" (Rom. 8:39).

And this triumph over hurt and death is not limited to
ourselves alone. In our relationship to Christ the Head, we
become related to all the other human beings who are
members of his body, the one holy catholic church.
Grasped by the living Christ, receiving forgiveness, we are
made part of his church. We must seek out the local
fellowship of this mystical fellowship, the communion of
the saints. In this communion we will find that God loves
not only us, but all human beings. We will find that Christ
lived, suffered, died, and rose to overcome the sins and to
heal the hurts of everyone. In our glimpse of eternity, we

will find that the sufferings of others whom we knew, now find their meaning also. The pathos that every mature person must feel when he/she remembers men and women he/she has known who suffered bitterly, can be eased now, for we know Christ loves those hurting ones who have no name, too.

The Revelation of Meaning

I wish to finish this discussion of where we hurt today on the same autobiographical note that began it. This is done not for self-advertisement, but out of honesty and to authenticate these observations.

I have suffered most of the hurts and anxieties we have examined together. No one can reach the fifth decade of life in the twentieth century without many opportunities to be hurt.

As a child I was frail and thin, the result of illness. I was poor, poor in a degree that is hard to imagine in the general prosperity America has known since World War II. As a teenager, I was shy and lonely, a loneliness made worse by being separated from my brother, sister, and parents. Reared apart from my family, in a strange environment, I was forced to become self-reliant and resolute, but with that growth came more loneliness and considerable unhappiness.

As I reached my seventeenth birthday, I struck out on my own, enlisting in the Marine Corps. That was in April, 1950. On June 25, 1950, the North Koreans invaded South Korea. I was in training camp. By August, I was on a troopship, combat-loaded in secrecy at the old Navy base in San Diego. After a month at sea, with a stubble of hair, huge pimples on my face, and two wisdom teeth trying to break through my gums, I went down the nets to land at Inchon. In the next month, the boys I played cards with across the Pacific were literally maimed and killed next to me. In November, we took ship North, landing at Wonson, North Korea. In the increasing cold we moved to the mountains of North Korea, headed toward Manchuria. On the night of November 25, 1950, the C.C.F., the Chinese Army, suddenly attacked and surrounded the First Marine Division, with which I served. The agony of the march back to the sea in the thirty-five below zero temperatures, harassed by several Chinese divisions, without adequate food, ammunition, and rest, has become part of American military history. I was seventeen years old, cold, uncertain, and fortunately, too stupid to be terrified. I remained in Korea for other campaigns in the south, leaving the front in July, 1951, as a casualty.

A simple story. Millions of others have suffered more. But my story has made me sensitive to human hurt. As a graduate student at the University of Chicago, I rebelled against the study of theology as an abstract discipline. I refused to see our study of the Bible, Christian history, and the thoughts of great Christians as an objective building of a system of thought to be taught. At a colloquy of faculty and students, I disturbed many by boldly saying (undoubtedly in an immature manner) that I could see no truth in any theology that was not an application of the healing, helping power of Christ to the hurts people suffer both in themselves and on behalf of others.

What, I asked then, and I ask now, has our religious outlook to say to the young man who grieves for the foot blown off by a land mine? What does Christ say to the peasant woman who, shot in the midriff, gave painful birth to a baby with a rifle round lodged in its poor little foot? I witnessed scenes like these by a cold roadside in Korea. What does God's power have to do with the grief I and others felt when we found Americans mutilated and murdered outside Seoul? What of the horror of the hundreds of

191

civilians shot and thrown in the Han River? Who in all the universe cares and feels for the men with frostbitten feet, for the prisoner, already wounded, shot out of hand?

I refused then, and I refuse now, to accept the philosopher Hegel's dictim that history is a slaughter bench upon which the Spirit is coming to consciousness in mankind. Man is neither God nor the devil, but sinner. Man is not despised by God, but loved and sought after. The wounded and the dead are not mistakes to be forgotten, but God's children who live in his memory. We need not hurt for them alone. Their suffering, and ours, is taken up in the sufferings of Christ, who, according to his glorious plan, is making all things, in heaven and on earth, one in himself. In Christ, all things take on meaning and every hurt is overcome and redeemed.

To me, the only answer to hurt, and the only theology worthy of the name, is expressed by that man who, as saint and sinner, lived with a thorn in his flesh and with Christ reigning in his heart:

He destined us in love to be his sons through Jesus Christ, according to the purpose of his will, to the praise of his glorious grace which he freely bestowed on us in the Beloved. In him we have redemption through his blood, the forgiveness of our trespasses, according to the riches of his grace which he lavished upon us. For he has made known to us in all wisdom and insight the mystery of his will, according to his purpose which he set forth in Christ, as a plan for the fulness of time, to unite all things in him, things in heaven and things on earth (Eph. 1:5–10).

Footnotes

Footnotes

Chapter 1.

1. Karl Menninger, *Whatever Became of Sin?* (New York: Hawthorn Books, 1973).
2. Janet Hitchman, *Such a Strange Lady* (New York: Avon Books, 1975) pp. 157–158.
3. Emil Brunner, *The Word of God and Modern Man* (Richmond: John Knox Press, 1964). Translated by David Cairns.
4. Wayne W. Dyer, *Your Erroneous Zones* (New York: Funk & Wagnalls, 1976); passim.
5. John Charles Cooper, *Fantasy and the Human Spirit* (New York: Seabury Press, 1975).
6. John C. Cooper and Rachel Conrad Wahlberg, *Your Exciting Middle Years* (Waco: Word Books, 1976).
7. Dyer, *op. cit.*
8. Theodore I. Rubin, *The Angry Book* (New York: Collier Books, 1970).
9. Gail Sheehy, *Passages: Predictable Crises of Adult Life* (New York: E. P. Dutton, 1976).
10. Information from "Down with Birthdays" by Jean Ayres Hartley, *Marathon World*, the publication of the Marathon Oil Company, No. 4, 1976, pp. 20–23, used by permission.
11. *Ibid.*
12. *Ibid.*
13. *Ibid.*
14. John Charles Cooper, *Religion After Forty* (Philadelphia: Pilgrim Press, 1973).
15. Cooper and Wahlberg, *op. cit.*
16. John Charles Cooper, *Finding a Simpler Life* (Philadelphia: Pilgrim Press, 1974).

Chapter 2.
1. Tom Wolfe, "The 'Me' Decade," *New York* magazine, Aug. 23, 1976, pp. 26ff.
2. Immanuel Kant, *Prolegomena to Any Future Metaphysics* (Library of Liberal Arts, 1950), p. 46.
3. *Ibid.*, p. 53.
4. *Ibid.*, pp. 55–56.

Chapter 3.
1. Louis Dupré, "The Religious Meaning of Mental Suffering," *The Christian Century*, Vol. XCIII, No. 12, April 7, 1976.
2. Otto Friedrich, *Going Crazy, An Inquiry into Madness in Our Time* (New York: Simon & Schuster, 1976).
3. Nathan Kline, *From Sad to Glad* (New York: Ballantine Books, 1974).

Chapter 4.
1. E.A. Robinson, "Richard Cory," *A Little Treasury of American Poetry*, edited by Oscar Williams (New York: Chas. Scribner's Sons, 1948).
2. Paul Tillich, *The Courage to Be* (New Haven: Yale University Press, 1952).
3. David Seabury, *How Jesus Heals Our Minds Today* (New York: Little, Brown & Co, 1950); passim. Used by permission.

Chapter 5.
1. Erich Fromm, *The Anatomy of Human Destructiveness* (New York: Holt, Rinehart & Winston, 1973).
2. Richard Andersen, "Living and Learning Forgiveness," *Learning With*, February, 1976, pp. 12–14.
3. Reinhold Niebuhr, *The Irony of American History* (New York: Chas. Scribner's Sons, 1952); p. 63.
4. Leslie H. Farber, *Lying, Despair, Jealousy, Envy, Sex, Suicide, Drugs, and the Good Life* (New York: Basic Books, 1976); passim.
5. *Ibid.*
6. Albert Schweitzer, *Reverence for Life* (New York: Harper & Row, 1969) p. 119.
7. Paul Tillich, *The New Being* (New York: Chas. Scribner's Sons, 1955) pp. 12–13.
8. Morton T. Kelsey, *Myth, History and Faith* (New York: Paulist Press, 1974) pp. 147–148.

Bibliography

Bibliography

Chapter 1.
Cooper, John Charles. *Religion After Forty* (Philadelphia: Pilgrim Press, 1973).
Cooper, John C., and Wahlberg, Rachel Conrad. *Your Exciting Middle Years* (Waco: Word Books, 1976).
Menninger, Karl, M.D., *Whatever Became of Sin?* (New York: Hawthorn Books, 1973).
Ruitenbeck, Hendrik M. *Psychotherapy: What It's All About* (New York: Avon Books, 1976).
Sheehy, Gail. *Passages, Predictable Crises of Adult Life* (New York: E. P. Dutton, 1976).
Wolfe, Linda. *Playing Around: Women and Extramarital Sex* (New York: William Morrow Co., 1975).

Chapter 2.
Bass, Howard L. and Rein, M. L. *Divorce or Marriage, A Legal Guide* (Englewood Cliffs, N.J.: Prentice-Hall, Inc., 1976).
Friedrich, Otto. *Going Crazy, An Inquiry Into Madness in Our Time* (New York: Simon & Schuster, 1976).
Laing, R. D. *The Divided Self* (New York: Pantheon Books, 1969).
Rubin, Theodore Isaac. *The Angry Book* (New York: Collier Books, 1970).
Rubin, Theodore Isaac. *Compassion and Self Hate* (New York: McKay, 1975).
Selye, Hans. *The Stress of Life* (New York: McGraw-Hill, 1976).

Chapter 3.
Dobson, James. *What Wives Wish Their Husbands Knew About Women* (Wheaton: Tyndale House, 1975).
Dyer, Wayne W. *Your Erroneous Zones* (New York: Funk & Wagnalls, 1976).
Fromm, Erich. *The Anatomy of Human Destructiveness* (New York: Holt, Rinehart & Winston, 1973).
Ginott, Haim G. *Between Parent and Child* (New York: Macmillan, 1968).
Greenberg, Samuel I. *Neurosis Is a Painful Style of Living* (New York: Signet Books, 1971).
Shedd, Charlie. *Talk to Me!* (Old Tappan, N.J.: Fleming H. Revell Co., 1976).
Snyder, Solomon H. *Madness and the Brain* (New York: McGraw-Hill, 1974).

Chapter 4.
Bontrager, John K. *Free the Child in You* (Philadelphia: Pilgrim Press, 1974).
Calhoun, Lawrence G. et. al, *Dealing With Crisis*, (Englewood Cliffs, N.J.: Prentice-Hall, Inc. 1976).
Deikman, Arthur. *Personal Freedom* (New York: Grossman Publishers, 1976).
DiCaprio, Nicholas S. *The Good Life* (Englewood Cliffs, N.J.: Prentice-Hall, 1976).
Gale, Raymond F. *Who Are You? The Psychology of Being Yourself* (Englewood Cliffs, N.J.: Prentice-Hall, 1976).
Greenwald, Jerry. *Be the Person You Were Meant to Be* (New York: Dell Publishing Co., 1974).
Harris, Sydney J. *The Authentic Person* (Niles, IL: Argus Communications, 1972).
Kline, Nathan S. *From Sad to Glad* (New York: Ballantine Books, 1974).
Kraus, C. Norman. *The Healing Christ* (Scottdale, PA: Herald Press, 1972).
Lakelin, Alan. *How to Get Control of Your Time and Your Life* (New York: Signet Books, 1973).
Lamott, Kenneth. *Escape From Stress* (New York: Berkley Medallion Books, 1975).
Lee, Dorothy. *Valuing the Self* (Englewood Cliffs, N.J.: Prentice-Hall, Inc. 1976).
May, Rollo. *The Courage to Create* (New York: W. W. Norton & Co., 1975).

Moorhead, Ted B. Jr. *How to Be a Family and Survive* (Waco: Word Books, 1976).

Newman, Mildred. and Berkowitz, Bernard. *How to Be Awake and Alive* (New York: Ballantine, 1975).

Newman, Mildred. and Berkowitz, Bernard. *How to Be Your Own Best Friend* (New York: Ballantine Books, 1971).

Oden, Thomas C. *Game Free, The Meaning of Intimacy* (New York: Harper & Row, 1974).

Osborne, Cecil. *Release from Fear and Anxiety* (Waco: Word Books, 1976).

Rosen, Gerald. *Don't Be Afraid* (Englewood Cliffs, N.J.: Prentice-Hall, 1976).

Schultz, William C. *Joy, Expanding Human Awareness* (New York: Grove Press, 1967).

Stringfellow, William. *Instead of Death* (New York: Seabury Press, 1976).

Chapter 5.

Becker, Ernest. *Escape From Evil* (New York: Free Press, 1975).

Elbin, Paul Nowell. *The Paradox of Happiness* (New York: Hawthorn, 1975).

Francoeur, Robert T. and Anna K. *The Future of Sexual Relations* (Englewood Cliffs, N.J.: Prentice-Hall, 1974).

Huxley, Laura A. *Between Heaven and Earth* (New York: Avon, 1976).

Huxley, Laura A. *You Are Not the Target* (New York, Avon, 1976).

Maltz, Maxwell. and Barker, Raymond C. *The Conquest of Frustration* (New York; Ballantine Books, 1969).

Kelsey, Morton T. *Myth, History and Faith* (New York: Paulist Press, 1974).

Kelsey, Morton T. *The Other Side of Silence* (Englewood Cliffs, N.J.: Paulist Press, 1976).

Naranjo, Claudio. *The Healing Journey* (New York: Ballantine Books, 1975).

Olson, Ken. *The Art of Hanging Loose in an Uptight World* (New York: Fawcett Crest Books, 1975).

Parrish, Louis. *No Pause At All* (New York: Reader's Digest Press, 1976).

Sloane, Valerie. *Creative Family Activities* (Nashville: Abingdon, 1976).

Spock, Benjamin. *Raising Children in a Difficult Time* (New York: W. W. Norton & Co., 1974).

Additional Resources

Becker, Ernest. *The Denial of Death* (New York: The Free Press, 1973).

Becker, Ernest. *The Structure of Evil* (New York: The Free Press, 1968).

Bower, Sharon A. and Bower, Gordon H. *Asserting Your Self* (Reading, MA: Addison-Wesley Publishing Co, 1976).

Ginandes, Shepard. M. D., *Coming Home* (New York: Delacorte Press, 1976).

Grollman, Earl A. *Talking About Death: A Dialogue Between Parent and Child* (Boston: Beacon Press, 1970).

Hite, Shere. *The Hite Report* (New York: Macmillan Co., 1976).

Jongeward, Dorothy and Scott, Dru. *Women As Winners* (Reading, MA: Addison-Wesley Publishing Co., 1976).

Kubler-Ross, Elisabeth. *On Death and Dying* (New York: Macmillan Co., 1969).

Offit, Avodah K., M. D. *The Sexual Self* (Philadelphia. J. B. Lippincott; 1977).

Robertiello, Richard C., M. D. *Hold Them Very Close, Then Let Them Go* (New York: Dial Press, 1975).

Safilios-Rothschild, Constantina. *Love, Sex, & Sex Roles* (Englewood Cliffs, N.J.: Prentice-Hall, Inc., 1977).

Wilt, Joy. *Happily Ever After* (Waco: Word Books, 1977).

Wolfe, Tom. *Mauve Gloves & Madmen, Clutter & Vine* (New York: Farrar, Straus & Giroux, 1976).

Zastrow, Charles, and Dae, Chang H., eds. *The Personal Problem Solver* (Englewood Cliffs, New Jersey: Prentice-Hall, 1977).

Zimbardo, Philip G. *Shyness: What It Is, What to Do About It*, (Reading, MA: Addison-Wesley Publishing Co., 1977).

Periodicals

Bender, N. Judson, M. D. "Marriage in the Middle Years." *Journal of the Louisiana State Medical Society*, Vol. 126, No. 9, Sept 1974.

Chamberlin, Leslie J., and Girona, Ricardo. "Our Children Are Changing." *Educational Leadership*, January 1976.

Dupré, Louis. "The Wounded Self: The Religious Meaning of Mental Suffering." *The Christian Century*, Vol. XCIII, No. 12, 7 April 1976.

"How Women Feel About Their Lives Today: A Survey of McCall's Readers." *McCall's Monthly Newsletter for Women*, "Right Now," April 1976.

McConnell, Theodore A. "The Course to Adulthood." *Journal of Religion and Health*, Vol. 5, No. 3, July 1966.

Novak, Michael. "The Family Out of Favor." *Harper's Magazine*, April 1976.

Wolfe, Tom. "The 'Me' Decade." *New York Magazine*, 23 August 1976.